CW00350727

Get started in Arabic

Frances Altorfer and
Mairi Smart

Hodder & Stoughton Ltd

338 Euston Road

London NW1 3BH

www.hodder.co.uk

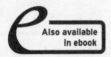
Also available in ebook

Contents

About the authors

Both authors are linguists of long experience and are familiar with the Arab countries, their society, religion and culture.

Frances Altorfer was born in England to a Swiss father and an English mother. She grew up in Kenya, where she developed her interest in languages by learning French, German and Russian at school and Swahili at home. Fran has lived in the Middle East, and travels regularly to the Gulf countries. She has many years of experience as a language teacher, using the most up-to-date teaching methods. She is co-author of several Arabic language books, including *Complete Arabic* (Hodder Education, 2010) and *Complete Spoken Arabic* (Hodder Education, 2010).

Mairi Smart was born in Cambridge to a family of linguists. Her father ignited her interest in Arabic, which she studied with German at university. She has lived in Egypt, Switzerland, Japan and the Arabian Gulf. A passionate linguist and teacher with almost 20 years' experience, Mairi has taught Arabic, German, French, Japanese and English to students of wide-ranging ages and abilities, using the latest interactive teaching methods. She is currently teaching Arabic in the United Arab Emirates.

Frances and Mairi firmly believe that it's never too late for you to learn a new language, and that speaking even a small amount helps you to connect with native speakers on a more personal level. Both Frances and Mairi encourage you to do this by making explanations within *Get Started in Arabic* as clear as possible, and by finding ways to make learning Arabic engaging and fun.

Introduction to the Arabic language

There are three main types of Arabic: **Classical Arabic**, **Modern Standard Arabic** and **Colloquial Arabic**.

The first, **Classical Arabic**, is the Arabic of the Holy Koran, or Qur'an. It is read and recited by millions of Muslims, many of whom are non-native Arabic speakers, all over the world, and has hardly changed since the first dictionary was written in the 8th century AD. This is quite amazing, considering that it would be impossible for the average person to read 8th century English nowadays. Classical Arabic is only used in the Qur'an and early poetry.

The second type is the modern written language, **Modern Standard Arabic** (MSA), and is hardly ever used in speech, except in formal situations such as news broadcasts or political speeches. Many Arabs believe that written Arabic is the only 'pure' Arabic, but no one speaks it and, in fact, even academics find it hard to keep speaking MSA for very long. So if you want to speak and understand Arabic, instead of only reading and writing it, you need to learn the third type, **Colloquial Arabic**, and this is the purpose of *Get Started in Arabic*.

The **Colloquial Arabic** spoken in daily life by nearly 300 million people is not just one language, but a series of dialects, varying widely from country to country, just as the English spoken in Scotland is different to the English spoken in Australia or Kentucky. These dialects fall into four or five main groups, and in this book you will learn the spoken Arabic of one of the larger groups, Gulf Arabic.

Gulf Arabic is spoken in the Arabian Peninsula and Iraq. Even within the Gulf region, there are differences from one country to another, but people still easily understand each other. For instance, in some regions, the word for *they go* is **yiruuHúun**, and in other parts the word used is **yirúuHuu**, without the final **-n**, but you will be understood whichever form you use. After you have worked through this book, you will have a good grounding in the basic features of Arabic and you will be able to adapt easily to the dialects of most other Arabic-speaking countries.

Colloquial Arabic is not often written down, except in cartoons and TV drama scripts or text messages between friends. In *Get Started in Arabic* we will show you how to read the MSA script so that you can understand common everyday signs and notices. Many people are put off by the apparently difficult script. In fact, this is one of the most rewarding aspects of learning Arabic, and once you have mastered all 28 letters, it is easy to read and write. Arabic is a highly phonetic language, i.e. it is written as it sounds, and has very few of the spelling oddities of English such as *write/right* or *cough/through*.

It is worth mentioning the influence of Islam on the Arabic language since this will be evident to you right from the start. Indeed, it is because of Islam that Arabic acquired the universal status which it has continued to enjoy since the Middle Ages, when it emerged as a world language. A rich and expressive language, Arabic plays an important part in preserving the culture of the Arabic-speaking people. The religious phrases and expressions that are introduced in this book are very widely heard, and can be used freely by Muslims and non-Muslims alike.

Arabs very much appreciate any attempt by a foreigner to learn their language, and your every effort will be greeted with amazement and enthusiasm. Knowledge of Arabic is the key to a society of very friendly people, which is often thought difficult to penetrate. Being able to speak even a little Arabic will enhance your social life, and, in the worlds of business or tourism, can open doors that would otherwise remain firmly closed.

We wish you every success as you embark on your Arabic journey and hope you will come to love the language, its people and their culture as much as we do.

How the units work

Conversations

Two conversations are provided within each unit. The first introduces the essential vocabulary and phrases of that unit, and the second develops the theme. All conversations are provided for you to listen to at your own pace; listen to these and repeat all of them, line by line, trying to mimic what you hear. When you become more confident, read the conversations out loud as you hear them, then cover up one part of the conversation and try to remember what to say.

Vocabulary

These sections contain key vocabulary and phrases to help you to understand the text and build up a useful base for further study. Practise saying the words and phrases out loud after listening to the audio. There are many ways of learning new vocabulary, but the most effective is to do something active with them rather than just look at the list of words. Try the Look, Cover, Say, Check method – i.e. look at the word, cover it up, say it out loud, check to see if you got it right!

Another method is to make a list of all the words from the unit that you find hard to remember, practise them two or three at a time, go and do something else, then come back to the list and see how many you can still remember. Then cross them off the list until you have none left.

Making your own flashcards is another great way to learn vocabulary, as well as become familiar with the Arabic alphabet. Write the word or letter in Arabic on one side, the English on the other, then turn them over one by one as you say them. Once you have mastered Arabic to English, try it the other way round, i.e. English face up, then try to say the Arabic.

The Discovery method – learn to learn!

There are lots of philosophies and approaches to language learning, some practical, some quite unconventional, and far too many to list here. Perhaps you know of a few, or even have some techniques of your own?

In this book, we have incorporated the **Discovery Method** of learning, a sort of DIY approach to learning. What this means is that you will be encouraged throughout the course to engage your mind and figure out the language for yourself, by identifying patterns, understanding grammar concepts, noticing words that are similar to English or similar to ones you have seen in earlier units, and more. This method promotes language awareness, a critical skill in acquiring a new language. As a result of your own efforts, you will be more able to retain what you have learned, use it with confidence, and – even better – apply those same skills to continuing to learn the language (or, indeed, another one) on your own after you've finished *Get Started in Arabic*.

Everyone can succeed in learning a language – the key is to know how to learn it. Learning is much more than just reading or memorizing grammar and vocabulary. It's about being an active learner, learning in real contexts and, most importantly, using what you've learned in different situations. Simply put, if you figure something out for yourself, you're more likely to understand it. And when you use what you've learned, you're more likely to remember it.

And because many of the essential but (let's admit it!) dull details, such as grammar rules, are taught through the **Discovery Method**, you'll have more fun while learning. Soon, the language will start to make sense and you'll be relying on your own intuition to construct original sentences independently, not just listening and repeating.

Enjoy yourself!

Exercises

The exercises in each unit provide you with an opportunity to practise the Arabic that you have learned. Answers to the exercises are given at the back in the Answer Key.

Note: to complete the listening exercises you will need to use the audio. To make your learning easier and more efficient, a system of icons indicates the actions you should take:

 This symbol indicates that the audio is needed for the following section.

 New words and phrases

 Listen and pronounce

 Figure something out for yourself

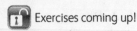 Exercises coming up!

 Culture tip

 Speak Arabic out loud

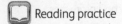 Reading practice

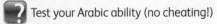 Test your Arabic ability (no cheating!)

Become a successful language learner

▶ Make a habit out of learning. Study a little every day – between 20 and 30 minutes, if possible. Gradually, the language will become clearer as your brain starts to make new connections. Just give yourself enough time, and you will succeed.

▶ Expand your language contact – try to take other opportunities to expose yourself to Arabic. As well as using this book, try listening to radio and television. If you listen to Arabic regularly, you'll find that you begin to 'tune in' to the language, and your vocabulary and language recognition will improve.

▶ Keep a notebook for vocabulary, and group words into topics, e.g., shopping, directions, etc., and don't worry too much about the spelling. Make a list of verbs as you come across them, in the form which is easiest for you to refer to later. Keep a separate section for pronunciation rules, and practice saying those words that trouble you.

▶ If you are listening to an Arabic speaker, try to guess what the key words are from the context. If you cannot get the gist of the conversation because of a word or phrase, repeat the word with a questioning tone; the speaker will probably paraphrase it, giving you the chance to understand it.

▶ Keep talking in Arabic. All language teachers will tell you that the successful learners are those who overcome their inhibitions and get into situations where they must speak and listen to the foreign language. Keep the conversations flowing, and don't worry about mistakes. Making mistakes is part of any normal learning process, but most mistakes are not serious and do not affect the meaning; concentrate on getting your message across. The most important thing to remember is BE BOLD!

The Arabic script

The Arabic script looks difficult because it is so different from what we are used to. In fact, the Arabic script is easy to master and with practice you will soon be able to distinguish the letters, as Arabic is generally written exactly as it sounds.

1 General facts about the Arabic script

▶ The basic Arabic alphabet has 28 letters.
▶ Arabic is written (and read!) from right to left – in the opposite direction to English.
▶ Like English handwriting, Arabic script is joined (or cursive); there is no equivalent of the text you are reading now, where all the letters have separate forms with spaces between them.
▶ Arabic has no capital letters.
▶ Six of the 28 letters do not join to the letter that follows.
▶ Arabic letters have four possible forms, depending on whether these are written on their own, or come at the beginning, in the middle or at the end of a word. This is because the joining strokes between the letters, called ligatures, slightly affect the shape of the letters on either side.
▶ The three long vowels **aa**, **ii** and **uu** are shown in the script.
▶ The three short vowels **a**, **i**, and **u** are not shown in the script. For example, the word **bank** (borrowed from English) is written **b-n-k**.

2 The alphabet

First, don't expect to take all this in at once. You can always come back to it again later. Pace your learning to suit yourself!

Throughout *Get Started in Arabic*, we introduce a few Arabic letters in each unit and have given the forms of each letter on their own, at the beginning, middle and end of a word. If you look at the letters carefully, you will see that there are generally only two shapes.

The Arabic alphabet is given here in its traditional order. Letters that are non-joiners are marked with an asterisk (*).

THE ARABIC LETTERS

Name	Beginning	Middle	End	On its own	Pronunciation
alif*	ا	ﺎ	ﺎ	ا	a
baa'	ﺑ	ﺒ	ﺐ	ب	b
taa'	ﺗ	ﺘ	ﺖ	ت	t
thaa'	ﺛ	ﺜ	ﺚ	ث	th
jiim	ﺟ	ﺠ	ﺞ	ج	j
Haa'	ﺣ	ﺤ	ﺢ	ح	H
khaa'	ﺧ	ﺨ	ﺦ	خ	kh
daal*	ﺩ	ﺪ	ﺪ	د	d
dhaal*	ﺫ	ﺬ	ﺬ	ذ	dh
raa'*	ﺭ	ﺮ	ﺮ	ر	r
zaay*	ﺯ	ﺰ	ﺰ	ز	z
siin	ﺳ	ﺴ	ﺲ	س	s
shiin	ﺷ	ﺸ	ﺶ	ش	sh
Saad	ﺻ	ﺼ	ﺺ	ص	S
Daad	ﺿ	ﻀ	ﺾ	ض	D
Taa'	ﻃ	ﻄ	ﻂ	ط	T
Dhaa'	ﻇ	ﻈ	ﻆ	ظ	DH
:ain	ﻋ	ﻌ	ﻊ	ع	:
ghain	ﻏ	ﻐ	ﻎ	غ	gh
faa'	ﻓ	ﻔ	ﻒ	ف	f
qaaf	ﻗ	ﻘ	ﻖ	ق	q
kaaf	ﻛ	ﻜ	ﻚ	ك	k
laam	ﻟ	ﻠ	ﻞ	ل	l
miim	ﻣ	ﻤ	ﻢ	م	m
nuun	ﻧ	ﻨ	ﻦ	ن	n
haa'	ﻫ	ﻬ	ﻪ	ه	h
waaw*	ﻭ	ﻮ	ﻮ	و	w
yaa'	ﻳ	ﻴ	ﻲ	ي	y

When we say the letter comes at the end, we mean that it is final after
a joining letter. If the letter before it is a non-joiner, then the separate
form is used. If you look closely, you can see that many final and separate
letters are stretched out, or have a 'flourish' after them.

This is what **baa'** looks like in its four forms – can you see the similarities?

Beginning	middle	End	on its own
ـبـ	ـبـ	ـب	ب

You can see that the basic form is the hook with a dot under it, the middle
shape has joining strokes before and after it, and the final form has an
elongation or flourish.

There is one combination consonant, called **laam-alif**. This is used when
this series of letters occurs, and it is a non-joiner:

Name	Beginning	Middle/End	On its own	Pronunciation
laam-alif	لا	ـلا	لا	laa

There is a letter called **taa' marbuutTah**, literally a 'bound' or 'tied' **taa'**.
This is the Arabic feminine ending which occurs at the end of words, so it
only ever has two forms: ending (after joiners) and on its own (after non-
joiners). It sounds like 'ah', which is how we have transcribed it. So look
out for words in this book ending in **-ah** – many of these will be feminine
nouns or adjectives.

Ending	On its own
ـة	ة

If you look at it carefully, you will see that it is a **haa'** with the two dots of
the **taa'** added. Sometimes **taa' marbuuTah** is 'untied' and regains its
taa' sound. But don't worry about this; we only mention it here because
you will come across it from time to time and may wonder what it is.
For example:

sayyáarah (*car*) becomes **sayyáarat al-mudíir** (*the manager's car*)

tádhkarah (*ticket*) becomes **tádhkarat dhiháab w iyáab** (*a return
ticket*)

VOWELS

The long vowels are expressed by the three letters **alif**, **waaw** and **yaa'**.

ا **alif** almost always expresses the vowel 'aa' as in *calm*.

و **waaw** expresses the vowel 'oo' as in *cool*, and can be the consonant w as in English *wish*

ي **yaa'** expresses the vowel 'ee' as in *keep*, and can be the consonant y as in English *yes*.

In Arabic writing, short vowels such as the *a* in *bat*, rather than the longer *a* in *calm*, are not usually marked except in the Holy Qur'an, schoolchildren's textbooks and ancient classical poetry. You will be introduced to the short vowels in the final unit of this book. Don't worry – rdng wtht shrt vwls snt s dffclt s y mght thnk!

Basically, it is better to think of the Arabic script as handwriting, since it is always cursive, no matter how it is produced. Because of this, calligraphy has become a highly developed art in the Arab world, and so there are more variations in the form of letters than you would find in English. In *Get Started in Arabic* we will help you to recognize the Arabic script, rather than to learn to write with it, and there are fuller descriptions of all the letters in each Unit. Arabic writing is fun to read. Look on it as an art form!

Abu Dhabi Beaches
Corniche | الـكورنيش

Pronunciation

Transliteration

Transliteration means expressing a language that uses a different writing system (like Arabic) in letters and symbols based on the Roman alphabet. There is no standard way of doing this, and we have tried to keep the system used in *Get Started in Arabic* as simple as possible.

The most important feature of a transliteration system is that it has an equivalent for every sound in the target language. This is different from conventional spelling. So, for example, in English the letter *s* has totally different sounds in the two words *loafs* and *loaves*, and the same *s* sound used in *loafs* can be spelled differently, as in *mince. Get Started in Arabic* is more or less restricted to the English alphabet, and we use capital letters to distinguish between Arabic sounds that seem related to non-Arabic speakers. For instance, Arabic has two sorts of **t**, which are distinguished like this: **tiin** means *figs*, and **Tiin** means *mud*. There is a full explanation of how to pronounce these sounds in the next section.

The Arabic sounds

The letters are given in standard Roman alphabet order, not in traditional Arabic order, so you can find the sounds more easily. The sound corresponding with the transliteration used in this book is given first, followed by the Arabic name for the letter. An example of the letter in an Arabic word is then followed by the English translation of the word.

We have divided the pronunciation guide into three groups:
▶ Group 1: Sounds that are more or less as in English.
▶ Group 2: Sounds that we don't have in English, but which are found in other European languages.
▶ Group 3: Sounds that are specific to Arabic.

GROUP 1

 00.01

b	baa'	as in **baab** *door*
d	daal	as in **dars** *lesson*
dh	dhaal	as in **dháalik** *that*
f	faa'	as in **fílfil** *pepper*
h	haa'	as in **húwwa** *he*
j	jiim	as in **jadíid** *new*
k	kaaf	as in **kabíir** *big*
l	laam	as in **laa** *not*, and it sometimes has a duller sound, as in English *alter*
m	miim	as in **múmkin** *possible*
n	nuun	as in **nuur** *light*
s	siin	as in **símsim** *sesame*
sh	shiin	as in **sharíi:ah** *sharia* (Islamic law)
t	taa'	as in **táajir** *merchant*
th	thaa'	as in **thaláathah** *three*
w	waaw	as in **wáaHid** *one*
y	yaa'	as in **yoom** *day*
z	zaay	as in **zooj** *husband*

GROUP 2

 00.02

r	raa'	as in **rájul** *man*. This is the trilled *r* of Scottish *very* ('verry'), and common in Italian and Spanish (*Parma, Barcelona*).
gh	ghain	as in **gharb** *west*. Similar to the *r* of Parisian French
kh	khaa'	as in **kháarij** *outside*. Like the sound of *ch* in Scottish *loch* and *och aye*

GROUP 3

 00.03

These sounds are specific to Arabic. To pronounce them requires practice and it is best to listen to native speakers if you can.

S, T, D, DH. With the exception of **H** (see below), the capitalized consonants are pronounced in a similar way to their small letter versions **s, t, d** and **dh**, except that the tongue is pressed down into a spoon shape and the sound is more forceful. These sounds have an effect on any surrounding vowels, which makes them sound more hollow. A rough (British) English equivalent is the difference in the *a* as in *Sam* and in *psalm*.

S	**Saad**	as in **Saghíir** *small*
T	**Taa'**	as in **Táalib** *student*
D	**Daad**	as in **Dayf** *guest*
DH	**DHaa'**	as in **DHuhr** *noon*

:   **:ain**   as in **:ámal** *work*. You will find that what is normally called gagging in English is actually a restriction in the deep part of the throat. If you begin to gag and then immediately relax the muscles in order to release the airstream from the lungs, you will have produced a perfect **:ain**.

H   **Haa'**   as in **Hajj** *pilgrimage*. Pronounced in exactly the same way as **:ain**, except that, instead of completely closing the muscles referred to above, they are just constricted and the air allowed to escape. The only time English speakers come near to a (weakish) **H** is when they breathe on their glasses before cleaning them. Both **:ain** and **Haa'** should always be pronounced with the mouth fairly wide open (say '*ah*').

'   **hamza**   as in **'ámal** *hope*. The **hamzah** or glottal stop occurs in English between words pronounced deliberately and emphatically (e.g. *She* (pause) *is* (pause) *awful!*), but is probably more familiar as the Cockney pronunciation of *t* or *tt* as in *bottle*. This sound is different from the **:ain**, and the difference affects the meaning. For instance, **'amal** means *hope*, but **:amal** means *work*.

q   **qaaf**   as in **qaríib** *near*. Officially pronounced as a 'back of the throat' English *c* or *k*, and not related to the *qu* in English. A rough equivalent is the pronunciation of the letter *c* in (British) English *calm*.

LOCAL VARIATIONS

Arabs from different regions throughout the Arab gulf pronounce some letters differently, so you may hear the following variations:

j	pronounced as y, e.g. **dajáaj** (*chicken*) = **dayáay**, and also as **g** or **j** as in French *Jacques*
dh and **DH**	pronounced as **d** or **z**
D	pronounced as **DH** in much of the Gulf.
k	sometimes pronounced as **ch** in parts of the Gulf e.g. **baakir** (*tomorrow*), or **baachir**.
q*	pronounced as a **g** in much of the Gulf

*In *Get Started in Arabic* we have introduced words containing **q** in both their Gulf and MSA forms, e.g. **garíib/qaríib** (*near*) and **suug/suuq** (*market*), but have listed them under **q** in the Vocabulary section (with both forms). In the **Go further** script sections, however, we have used the standard Arabic **q** transliteration only to help you link the sound with the written letter **qaaf**, i.e. **suuq** (market) appears only as **suuq** and not as **suug**.

VOWELS

 00.04 There are only five common vowel sounds, three of which occur both long and short. These have been transcribed as follows:

aa	as in **tháalith** *third*, a long emphatic *a* as in the word *and* in: '*Did he really eat a whole chicken?*' '*Yes, <u>and</u> he ate a steak as well!*'
a	as in **ábadan** *never*, roughly as in *hat*
ii	as in **kabíir** *big*, like *Eve* and French *livre*
i	as in **jíbin** *cheese*, like *big*
uu	as in **filúus** *money*, like *rude*, French *vous*, or German *Schule*
u	as in **buldáan** *countries*, like *put* (never as in *cup*)
oo	as in **tilifóon** *telephone*, like *rose* pronounced in Scotland, or French *beau*
ai	as in **bait** *house*, like *wait*

You also hear this last pair of vowels:

ay	as in **dubáy** *Dubai*, like *aye*

xviii

DOUBLED CONSONANTS

00.05 These must be pronounced clearly twice in Arabic. Imagine a sort of hyphen between them. One example should make this clear:

Hamaam means *pigeons*

Hammaam means *bath* or *bathroom*.

STRESS

00.06 The best way to learn where the stress in each new word falls is to listen to the audio as often as you can, and practise saying the words and phrases out loud. Listening to native Arabic speakers and Arab TV and radio as much as possible will also help you 'get your ear in'.

One simple general rule, however, is that if a word contains a long vowel (**aa**, **ii** or **uu**), the stress falls on this; and if there is more than one (long vowel), the stress falls on the one nearest the end of the word:

makáatib but **makaatíib**

The stress will be on the last long syllable before a vowel ending.

To help you get used to where the stress falls, the stressed syllables of words have been marked with an accent: **á**, **áa**, etc. in the first seven units.

PRONUNCIATION OF 'AL-' (*THE*)

In Arabic writing, **al-** (*the*) never stands alone as it does in English. It is always attached to another word. Although it never changes in writing, **al-** has one peculiarity. If the word it is joined to begins with one of the following fourteen letters:

t, th, d, dh, r, z, s, sh, S, D, T, DH, l, n

the 'l' (**laam**) of **al-** is dropped in speech and the first letter of the word it is attached to is clearly doubled.

These particular letters are known as Sun letters, simply because the word **shams** (*sun*) begins with **shiin**, which is one of them. The remaining letters are known as Moon letters because **qámar** (*moon*), begins with **qaaf** which is not a Sun letter.

For example, we write and say **al-kuwáit** (**kaaf** is not a Sun Letter), but we write **al-sháarjah** and say **ash-sháarjah** (**shiin** is a Sun letter). You can see that in **ash-sháarjah** the **shiin** is doubled. We have shown this in the transliteration in this book. It is an important point of pronunciation and you must pronounce the doubled versions of the letters listed above clearly. With practice, you will soon be doing this without thinking.

This photograph shows the inconsistent transliteration of Arabic signs. The correct pronunciation is **as-suuq** or **as-suug** in Gulf Arabic.

 Look at the following words and phrases. Do the words following al- begin with Sun or Moon letters? (Note: there are two answers for d and f.)

   a   SabáaH al-kháir (*good morning*)
   b   SabáaH an-núur (*good morning to you too*)
   c   al-kuwáit (*Kuwait*)
   d   ar-rúba: al-kháali (*the Empty Quarter*)
   e   as-sa:udíyyah (*Saudi*)
   f   ash-sharq al-áwsaT (*the Middle East*)
   g   ash-shamáal (*the North*)
   h   al-khalíij (*the Gulf*)
   i   as-saláamu :aláikum (*hello*)
   j   al-imaaráat (*the Emirates*)

> **TIP**
> 'The Empty Quarter' is a vast area of desert in the south of the Arabian Peninsula.

 00.07 **Listen and repeat.**

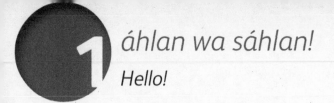

áhlan wa sáhlan!

Hello!

In this unit you will learn how to:
▶ *say* hello *and* goodbye.
▶ *use common greetings.*
▶ *introduce yourself and others.*
▶ *say where you're from.*
▶ *ask someone where they are from.*

CEFR: (A1) *Can establish basic social contact by saying where he or she is from and by using simple everyday polite forms of greetings, farewells and introductions.*

The Arabian Gulf

The Arabic you will learn in this book is called Gulf Arabic, the language spoken in **al-khalíij al-:árabi** (*the Arabian Gulf*). This region includes the land that extends from **al-:iráaq** (*Iraq*) in **ash-shamáal** (*the North*) to **al-yáman** (*Yemen*) in **al-janúub** (*the South*) and from **al-mámlakah al-:arabíyyah as-sa:udíyyah** (*the Kingdom of Saudi Arabia*), also known simply as **as-sa:udíyyah**, in the West to **:umáan** (*Oman*) in the East.

The Arabian Gulf is an important region in **ash-sharg al-áwsaT** (*the Middle East*). **:árabi** (*Arabic*) – or more formally **al-lúghah al-:arabíyyah** (*the Arabic language*), which is spoken in **al-khalíij** – varies slightly from country to country, but the language introduced in this book is widely understood throughout the region. From the skyscrapers and opulent malls of **dubáy** (*Dubai*) to the desert wilderness of **ar-rub: al-kháali** (*the Empty Quarter*), **al-khalíij** is truly a region of contrasts with something for everyone.

What is the Arabic word for *language*?

2

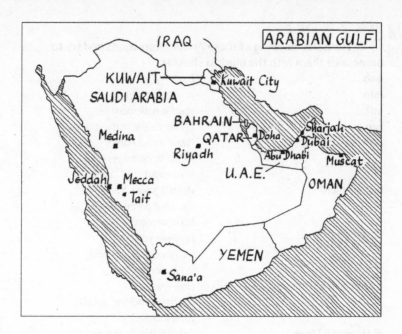

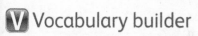 Vocabulary builder

GREETINGS AND GOODBYES

In Arabic, it is very important to be able to greet people, to reply appropriately when someone greets you, and to say goodbye.

01.01 Look at these words and phrases, then listen and practise these sounds by imitating the pronunciation of the speakers.

SabáaH al-kháir	*good morning*
SabáaH an-núur	*good morning* (only used in reply to **SabáaH al-kháir**)
masáa' al-kháir	*good afternoon/evening*
masáa' an-núur	*good afternoon/evening* (reply to **masáa' al-kháir**)
má:a s-saláamah	*goodbye* (reply is the same)

> **PRONUNCIATION TIP**
> Remember to pronounce the stress where marked!

1 *áhlan wa sáhlan! Hello!*   3

NEW EXPRESSIONS

01.02 **Note the meaning of these Arabic expressions and try to pronounce them with the marked stresses.**

ána ...	*I ...*
ínta	*you (to a man)*
ínti	*you (to a woman)*
ísm-i...	*My name (lit. name-my ...) ...*
aish ísm-ak?	*What's your name?*
	(lit. what name-your?)
	(to a man)
aish ísm-ich?	*What's your name?*
	(lit. what name-your?)
	(to a woman)
kaif Háal-ak?	*How are you?*
	(lit. how condition-your?)
	(to a man)
kaif Háal-ich?	*How are you?*
	(lit. how condition-your?)
	(to a woman)
al-Hámdu li-l-láah	*fine (lit. thanks to God)*
bi-kháir	*well*
wa	*and*
wa ínta?	*And you?*
	(to a man)
wa ínti?	*And you?*
	(to a woman)
ínta min wain?	*Where are you from?*
	(lit. you from where?)
	(to a man)
ínti min wain?	*Where are you from?*
	(lit. you from where?)
	(to a woman)
ána min dubáy	*I (am) from Dubai*

> **PRONUNCIATION TIP**
> Some word endings differ when speaking to a man or a woman. Make sure your endings are clear so as not to offend!

4

Hiwaar 1 *Conversation 1*

01.03 *At a business meeting in Abu Dhabi, Mohammed talks to Laila, another participant. Listen first, then answer the question.*

1 What time of day is it?

Mohammed	SabáaH al-kháir.
Laila	SabáaH an-núur. aish ísm-ak?
Mohammed	ána ísm-i muHámmad. wa ínti, aish ísm-ich?
Laila	ána ísm-i laila.
Mohammed	kaif Háal-ich?
Laila	al-Hámdu li-l-láah, bi-kháir. wa ínta, kaif Háal-ak?
Mohammed	al-Hámdu li-l-láah.
Laila	ínta min wain?
Mohammed	ána min dubáy. wa ínti?
Laila	ána min ábu DHábi.

AL-HÁMDU LI-L-LÁAH

The expression **al-Hámdu li-l-láah** never changes and is used in many situations. Even if their arm has just dropped off, the devout Muslim will still use this phrase when asked how they are!

---

2 What do you think? Read the conversation and answer the following questions.
   a Does Mohammed know Laila?
   b Where does Mohammed come from?

3 Match the Arabic to its correct English meaning.

a	SabáaH al-kháir	**1**	My name is
b	aish ísm-ich?	**2**	fine (lit. thanks to God)
c	ána ísm-i	**3**	Good morning.
d	kaif Háal-ak?	**4**	What's your name?
e	al-Hámdu li-l-láah	**5**	How are you?

4 01.03 **Now listen again line by line and try to imitate the speakers. Pay careful attention to the pronunciation and notice where the stress is on each word.**

Language discovery

 a **Look at these phrases. What do you notice about the way** *is* **and** *are* **are said in Arabic?**

aish ísm-ak?

ána ísm-i muHámmad

ána min dubáy

b Two different words for *you* are used in the conversation: ínta and ínti. Why?

c Find the word ism- throughout the conversation. How many different endings does it have, and what are these?

1 *IS* AND *ARE*

In Arabic there is no equivalent of the verb *to be* in the present tense. English sentences containing the words *is* or *are* are formed in Arabic as follows:

ána ísm-i joon	*My name is John.* (lit. *I name-my John.*)
aish ísm-ak?	*What is your name?* (lit. *What name-your?*)
kaif Háal-ak?	*How are you?* (lit. *How condition-your?*)
ínta min amríika?	*Are you from America?* (lit. *You from America?*)

al-Hiin dáwr-ak! *Now your turn!*

How would you say what your name is in Arabic?

2 PRONOUNS: *I* AND *YOU* (TO A MAN AND TO A WOMAN)

A pronoun is a word that refers to a person or a thing, such as *I*, *you*, *he*, *she* or *it*. Instead of saying *Jane is from England*, we can use a pronoun to replace the name *Jane*, and say *She is from England*.

The word **ána** always means *I*, whether you are male or female. However, in Arabic there is a very clear distinction when saying *you* to a man or woman. To say *you* to a man use **ínta**, and to a woman say **ínti**.

ínta min al-kuwáit?	*(Are) you from Kuwait?* (to a man)
laa, ána min al-imaaráat	*No, I (am) from the Emirates.*
ínti min ustráalya?	*(Are) you from Australia?* (to a woman)
ná:am, ána min sídni!	*Yes, I ('m) from Sydney!*

> **TIP**
> laa — *no*   ná:am (also áywa) — *yes*

al-Hiin dáwr-ak! *Now your turn!*

So, how do you say *I am from Australia*?

3 POSSESSIVE PRONOUNS: *MY* AND *YOUR*

Possessives describe *who* or *what* something belongs to. In English we use the words *my*, *your*, *his* and *hers*. To say *my* and *your* in Arabic we add an ending (called a suffix) to the person or thing being possessed. The endings in the conversation you have just heard are:

-i	*my*	**ísm-i** *my name* (lit. *name-my*)
-ak	*your* (to a man)	**ísm-ak** *your name* (lit. *name-your*, to a man)
-ich	*your* (to a woman)	**ísm-ich** *your name* (lit. *name-your*, to a woman)

> **PRONUNCIATION TIP**
> The feminine pronoun ending **-ich** is the most common pronunciation in the Gulf, but you may also hear **-ik** or even **-ish**, as in **kaif Háal-ish** (*How are you?* to a woman).

PRACTICE 1

1 Complete each sentence by adding the correct word(s).

> **gáTar   Háal-ich   ísm-i   min**

- **a** ána _____ jaimz (*James*).
- **b** ána _____ iskutláanda.
- **c** áHmad min _____.
- **d** kaif _____?

> **TIP**
> | iskutláanda | Scotland |
> | gáTar (qáTar) | Qatar |

2 First read, then add the missing Arabic words. Don't forget to check whether the endings are masculine or feminine!

> Alice   masáa' al-kháir.
> Jim   masáa' an-núur. aish ísm-_____?
> Alice   ána ísm-_____ áalis. wa _____, aish ism-_____?
> Jim   ána ísm-i jim.
> Alice   kaif Háal-_____?
> Jim   al-Hámdu li-l-láah, bi-kháir. wa _____?

3 Complete each sentence by adding the correct word from those supplied in the box. Careful – there are two words you won't need!

ísm-ak kaif ínta ísm-i
Háal-ich ána min

a ána _____ záinab.
b aish _____?
c _____ ísm-i Hámad.
d _____ min wain?
e kaif _____?

🎧 Listen and understand

1 01.04 **Listen to these people telling you their names and where they are from. Match the correct place to each person.**

a	Khalid	**1**	London, England
b	Ahmed al-Qasimi	**2**	Abu Dhabi in the Emirates
c	James Smith	**3**	Oman
d	Dalya	**4**	New York
e	Karen McGregor	**5**	Saudi Arabia
f	Zainab al-Loozi	**6**	Bahrain

2 01.05 **Listen to these speakers, then say if they are talking to a man or a woman.**

a m/f		**b** m/f		**c** m/f	
d m/f		**e** m/f		**f** m/f	

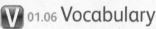

01.06 Vocabulary

as-saláamu :aláikum	hello (lit. *peace be on you*)
wa :aláikum as-saláam	hello (lit. *and on you be peace* - only used in reply to as-saláamu :aláikum)
áhlan wa sáhlan	hello/welcome
áhlan bii-k/bii-ch	hello/welcome (m/f) (reply to áhlan wa sáhlan)

> **PRONUNCIATION TIP**
> The **-a** of **wa** (*and*) often slides into the next word if the next word starts with a vowel, so **wa :aláikum as-saláam** becomes **w :aláikum as-saláam**. Try it for yourself!

Hiwáar 2 *Conversation 2*

01.07 Mohammed and Laila meet again later. Mohammed introduces his friends Mark and Sara.

1 Read as you listen. Which countries are Mark and Sara from?

Laila	as-saláamu :aláikum.
Mohammed	w :aláikum as-saláam. kaif Háal-ich yaa láila?
Laila	al Hámdu li-l-lah.
Mohammed	háadha mark, húwwa min lándan fii ingiltarra. wa háadhi sáarah, híyya min amríika.
Laila	áhlan wa sáhlan.
Mark and Sara	áhlan bii-ch.

> **YAA**
> In Arabic, the word **yaa** is usually used when addressing someone by name.

2 Which city is Mark from?

3 Match the Arabic to the English.

a	híyya min amríika	1	hello/welcome
b	háadha	2	this (f)
c	húwwa min lándan	3	she (is) from America
d	háadhi	4	this (m)
e	áhlan wa sáhlan	5	he (is) from London

Language discovery

 1 Find the words **húwwa** and **híyya** in the conversation – which means *he* and which means *she*?

2 Mohammed used the words **háadha** and **háadhi** to introduce Mark and Sara. What do you think these words mean?

1 MORE PRONOUNS – *HE* AND *SHE*

You have already learned how to say *I*, and *you* to a man and a woman. Here are two more pronouns: *he* and *she*.

| húwwa | he | mark min lándan → húwwa min lándan | He (is) from London. |
| híyya | she | sáarah min amríika → híyya min amríika | She (is) from America. |

2 HOW TO SAY *THIS*

In Arabic, the words **háadha** and **háadhi** are also pronouns and mean *this*.

háadha   *this* (masculine)   **háadhi**   *this* (feminine)

They can also be used to make sentences since there is no verb *to be* in Arabic.

háadha fáysal   *This (is) Faisal.*

háadhi náadiya   *This (is) Nadia.*

 PRACTICE 2

1 Complete each sentence with either **húwwa** or **híyya** to say where each person is from.

   a muHámmad: _____ min al-baHráin.

   b ánya: _____ min bríTáaniya.

   c fáaTimah: _____ min ash-shárjah.

   d jaak: _____ min faránsa.

2 First read the following about Ahmed, then imagine that you are talking about Fatima. Now change each sentence from masculine to feminine.

   a háadha áHmad.

   b húwwa min ábu DHábi?

   c laa, húwwa min gáTar

3 01.08 **Listen to these speakers introduce their friends. Say if each friend is male or female.**

a háadha iqbáal   **d** háadhi jamíilah

b háadha tamíim   **e** háadhi sáarah

c háadha :áadil   **f** háadhi imrán

4 01.09 **Now introduce the following people and say where each is from.**

Example: a háadha málik, húwwa min másqat.

a málik (m) – másqat (Muscat)

b náasir (m) – jáddah (Jeddah)

c híbah (f) – al-yáman (Yemen)

d maría (f) – isbáanya (Spain)

Go further

READING ARABIC

The Arabic word for *the* is **al-** and it is written like this in Arabic:

ال...   **al-**   *the*

It is always attached to the word that follows it and is written with two letters, **alif** (ا) and **laam** (ل). **al-** is easy to recognize, as it always comes at the beginning of a word: ال... as you can see in the following examples. Remember, Arabic script is read from right to left!

| الخليج | **al-khalíij** | *the* Gulf |
| اليمن | **al-yáman** | Yemen |

In English the names of some countries have *the* in front of them, such as the Netherlands and the USA. It is the same in Arabic but there are more of them, and they aren't always translated in English, as in Yemen. For example, **al-baHráin** (lit. *the Bahrain*) is just known as *Bahrain* in English.

> **WHAT'S IN A NAME?**
> Do you know what **al-baHráin** means? **báHar**, or **baHr**, means *sea* and **-ain** means *two* of anything – so when you add them together **al-baHráin** means *the two seas*, which describes its setting in the Arabian Gulf beautifully.

> **PRONUNCIATION TIP**
> Remember that if the name of the country begins with a Sun letter, the **l** of **al-** disappears, and the first letter must be doubled! (See Pronunciation guide.)

The letters **alif** and **laam** also appear separately. **alif** often has a small figure called a **hamza** (which looks like a backwards figure two) above or below it. If it is above the **alif** it makes it sound like **a** as in the name **Ahmed**, or an **u** as in **ukht** (*sister*). If the **hamza** is below the **alif**, it sounds like **i**, as in the word **ingiltárra**. **alif** is one of the six non-joiners, i.e. it doesn't join to the following letter. Here are **alif** and **laam** in their different positions.

end of a word	middle of a word	start of a word	alone
سينما **síinma** *cinema*	سارة **sáarah** *Sara* (girl's name)	أحمد **áHmad** *Ahmed* (boy's name) إنجليزي **ingíizi** *English* أخت **ukht** *sister*	ا **alif** أ إ
مول **mool** *mall*	خليج **khalíij** *gulf*	ليمون **laimóon** *lemon*	ل **laam**

Did you spot the laam in the middle of the word khalíij?

1 **Find three countries in the following list that begin with ... الـ (al-)** (*the*) **in Arabic.**

	Arabic	English
1	الكويت	Kuwait
2	قطر	Qatar
3	العراق	Iraq
4	السودان	Sudan
5	عمان	Oman

2 01.10 **First listen to the pronunciation of these Arab countries, then practise saying them by imitating the speakers.**

as-sudáan	al-:iráaq
:umáan	al-baHráin
al-yáman	qáTar

3 **The word ... ال (al-) is very common in street names. Can you find it in these Dubai street signs?**

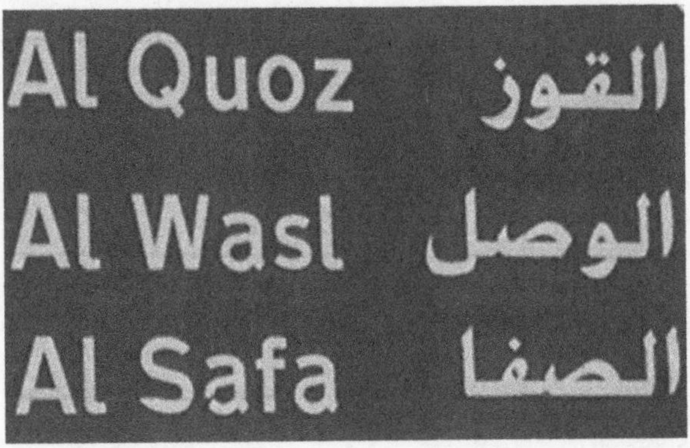

PRONUNCIATION TIP

The correct pronunciation of **al Safa** would be **aS-Safa** since **Saad** is a Sun letter.

Test yourself

1 Give your own response to each greeting/question, taking care with your pronunciation.

   a as-saláamu :aláikum

   b masáa' al-kháir

   c aish ísm-ak/ísm-ich?

   d ínta/ínti min wain?

   e má:a s-saláamah

> **TIP**
> You will find a range of countries in the glossary.

2 01.11 What is the missing word in each phrase?

   a as-saláamu _____

   b áhlan _____ sáhlan

   c húwwa _____ briTáaniya

   d _____ ísm-i máaykil (Michael)

   e _____ an-núur

   f _____ Háal-ak?

   g _____ fiyóona smiith

3 What questions would you ask to get these replies?

   a Speaker 1: _____

      Speaker 2: ána ísm-i náadiya.

   b Speaker 1: _____

      Speaker 2: ána ísm-i Hámad.

   c Speaker 1: _____(to a man)

      Speaker 2: al-Hámdu li-l-láah, w ínta?

SELF CHECK

I CAN. . .

○	... say *hello* and *goodbye*.
○	... use common greetings.
○	... introduce myself and others.
○	... say where I'm from.
○	... ask someone where they are from.

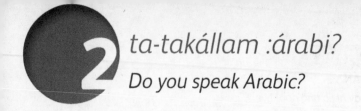

ta-takállam :árabi?

Do you speak Arabic?

In this unit you will learn how to:
▶ *state your nationality.*
▶ *say what languages you speak.*
▶ *recognize and use numbers from 0–10.*
▶ *ask for and give telephone numbers.*
▶ *ask for someone on the telephone.*

CEFR: (A1) *Can ask for and provide personal information and can use numbers effectively.*

 ## Arabic numbers

Any attempt to speak **:árabi** (*Arabic*) is met with delight. Arabs are very interested in visitors who can speak even a few words of their language, so being able to say a little about yourself in Arabic, such as your **jinsíyyah** (*nationality*), will be well received.

During the Middle Ages the Arabs passed the torch of Classical learning to Western scholars. The Arabs introduced the simpler decimal system that we use today, and spread the concept of **Sifir** (*zero* or *cipher*). There are many other words used in English, such as *algebra* and *algorithm*, which are Arabic in origin. It is useful to know Arabic numerals when you are out and about in the Gulf to help you deal confidently with such things as prices and telephone numbers.

Arabs have taken to the mobile **tilifóon** culture with great enthusiasm. It is common for people to have several mobile phones, even speaking into two at once! Everyone is eager to give their **rágam tilifóon** (*phone number*) to a new acquaintance so they can get in touch at any time.

 Look at these Arabic numbers. Can you work out what they are?

٩   ٣   ١   ٢

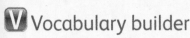 Vocabulary builder

AL-JINSIYYÁAT W AL-LUGHÁAT
NATIONALITIES AND LANGUAGES

 1 02.01 **Match each nationality in Arabic to its English translation.**

a	sá:udi	1	French
b	imaráati	2	British
c	inglíizi	3	American
d	briTáani	4	English
e	faránsi	5	Saudi
f	amríiki	6	Emirati
g	ayrlánda	7	Irish

 Now cover up the Arabic. Can you say the Arabic words again without looking?

2 **What are these languages in English?**

a	:árabi	c	isbáani
b	inglíizi	d	faránsi/faransáawi

> **AL-LÚGHAH AL-:ARABÍYYAH**
>
> The formal name for the Arabic language is **al-lúghah al-:arabíyyah**. As **al-lúghah** is a feminine word, the word describing it must also be feminine, but most often people just use the word **:árabi** (*Arabic*). Similarly, English becomes **inglíizi**.

NEW EXPRESSIONS

 02.02 **Can you add the missing meanings in English?**

min fáDHl-ak	*please* (to a man)
min fáDHl-ich	*please* (to a woman)
shúkran	*thank you*
:áfwan	*you're welcome* (reply to above)
shwáyya shwáyya	*slowly* (lit. *a little a little*)
:an idhn-ak	*excuse me* (to a man)
:an ídhn-ich	*excuse me* (to a woman)
a-takállam :árabi	*I speak* _____
maa a-takállam inglíizi	*I don't speak* _____
ta-takállam inglíizi?	*Do you* (to a man) *speak* _____?
ta-takállam-íin inglíizi?	*Do you* (to a woman) *speak* _____?
wáajid (also wáayid) zain	*very good/very well*
shwáyya	*a little*

bass	only/enough
ínta baHráin-i?	Are you Bahraini? (m)
ána miSr-íyyah	I am Egyptian (f)
áasif	I'm sorry (man speaking)
áasifah	I'm sorry (woman speaking)

 Hiwaar 1 *Conversation 1*

02.03 *In Abu Dhabi, Lauren and Alex get talking to Nasser. First listen and follow the text. Then answer the question.*

1 What nationality is Nasser?

Lauren	:an ídhn-ak, ta-takállam inglíizi?
Nasser	laa, áasif, a-takállam :árabi bass. ínti ingliz-íyyah?
Lauren	laa, ána amrik-íyyah. w ínta?
Nasser	ána imaráat-i. ta-takállam-íin :árabi wáajid zain!
Lauren	(*laughs*) laa, laa, shwáyya bass. háadha aliks, húwwa briTáan-i.
Nasser	áhlan wa sáhlan.
Alex	áhlan biik.

> **BASS!**
>
> **bass** is a very useful little word with a number of meanings. Depending on the context, it can mean *just*, *enough*, *stop* or *but*.

al-Hiin dáwr-ak! *Now your turn!*

You are reversing your car when someone behind you shouts *bass!* What should you do?

  a go slower

  b go faster

  c hit the brakes immediately!

2 Read the conversation again, then answer these questions.

  a What does Lauren ask Nasser first?

  b What languages does Nasser speak?

  c What does Nasser say about Lauren's Arabic?

  d What is the Arabic word for *no*?

  e Who is American?

  f Who is British?

3 02.03 **Listen again, then decide which statements are true (T)
and which are false (F).**

   a Nasser speaks English.

   b Lauren is American.

   c Nasser is Qatari.

 4 02.03 **Listen again, this time taking the part of Lauren.**

Language discovery

 1 Look at these expressions from the conversation.

Nasser:	ána imaráat-i
Lauren:	ána amrik-íyyah

Why do they use different endings for their nationalities?

2 What is the Arabic for these phrases?

   a I speak

   b you speak (m)

   c you speak (f)

1 NATIONALITY ADJECTIVES

In Arabic, words describing nationality are usually formed by adding
a masculine or feminine ending to the name of the country. For most
nationalities you add:

-i for a man   **-íyyah** for a woman

gáTar *Qatar* → **gáTar-i** *Qatari* (m) or **gaTar-íyyah** *Qatari* (f)

If the name of a country ends in **-a** or **-ah**, this is left off before the
ending is added:

briTáaniya *Britain* → **briTáan-i/briTan-íyyah** *British*

faránsa *France* → **faráns-i/farans-íyyah** *French*

But use:

ingiltárra *England* → **inglíiz-i/ingliz-íyyah** *English*

If the place name in Arabic has **al-** the in front of it, this is left out.

al-baHráin *Bahrain* → **baHráin-i/baHrain-íyyah** *Bahraini*

as-sudáan *Sudan* → **sudáan-i/sudaan-íyyah** *Sudani*

2 I SPEAK, YOU SPEAK

In English, verb forms are all the same, regardless of the subject (e.g. *I speak, you speak*) with the exception of *he/she speaks*. In Arabic the verb changes slightly, depending on the subject.

(ána) a-takállam	*I speak*
(ínta) ta-takállam	*you* (m) *speak*
(ínti) ta-takallam-íin	*you* (f) *speak*

> **PRONOUNS**
> Pronouns are not always used, since the verb form indicates the subject. You will learn more about this in Unit 3.

PRACTICE 1

1 Are these nationalities masculine or feminine?

a imaráat-i
b alman-íyyah
c ustráal-i
d ingliz-íyyah
e baHrain-íyyah
f faráns-i
g kuwáit-i
h irland-íyyah

> **TIP**
> **almáani** *German* (m)

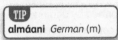

2 Make each sentence feminine, as shown in the example. Remember to change the pronouns (*you, he*) where necessary.

Example: a ána ingliz-íiyyah min lándan

a ána inglíiz-i, min lándan.
b ínta iTáal-i?
c húwwa :umáan-i.
d húwwa sudáan-i.
e ána briTáan-i, min iskutlánda.
f ínta gáTar-i?

3 Now translate the sentences in question 2 into English.

4 Who's talking? Look at the following phrases, then match them to the correct image.

1   2   3

a a-takállam inglíizi

b a-takallam faránsi

c a-takállam :árabi

 5 Complete the conversation between Khalid and Jim by adding the most appropriate words from those supplied.
Speak out loud.

| shwáyya | inglíiz-i | wáajid zain |
| laa, laa | ínta | min |

Khalid   _____ amríik-i?
Jim   laa, ána _____
Khalid   ínta _____ lándan?
Jim   _____, ána min máanshistr!
Khalid   ta-takállam :árabi _____!
Jim   laa, _____ bass.

Listen and understand

 1 02.04 First listen, then repeat these useful expressions out loud. Do this several times until you are confident with your pronunciation.

a min fáDHlak
b shúkran
c :áfwan
d :an ídhnik
e wáajid zain
f shwáyya

2 02.05 Listen to each person stating their nationality. Who's talking? What are their nationalities?

1   2   3

4   5   6

a _____
b _____
c _____
d _____
e _____
f _____

 3 Now Look at the pictures in 2 again, then state their nationalities in Arabic. Start with 'ána...'

02.06 Listen twice to the speaker count from zero to 10, then repeat after the speaker.

Arabic numeral	Arabic pronunciation	English
.	Sífir	0
١	wáaHid	1
٢	ithnáin	2
٣	thaláathah	3
٤	árba:ah	4
٥	khámsah	5
٦	síttah	6
٧	sáb:ah	7
٨	thamáan(i)yah	8
٩	tís(a):ah	9
١٠	:ásharah	10

ARABIC NUMBERS

In Arabic, numbers are written from left to right in the same direction as English, e.g. ١٩٢٤ = 1924. Some countries now use the same form we use (1, 2, 3, etc) and this practice is spreading.

 NEW EXPRESSIONS

 02.07

kam rágam tilifóon-ak/-ich?	*What (is) your phone number?*
rágam tilifóon-i ...	*My phone number is ...*
márrah tháaniyah	*again (lit. a second time)*

PRONUNCIATION TIP

Be aware that you will hear both **rágam** and **ráqam**, and even **ragm** or **raqm**.

ASKING FOR PEOPLE ON THE TELEPHONE

To ask for someone on the telephone, simply say … (i.e. the name of the person you want) **mawjúud?** This is the standard way of asking if someone is available. As **mawjúud** is an adjective describing a person or thing, it agrees in gender so if the person you want is a woman, it becomes **mawjúud-ah**.

:abd al-:azíiz mawjúud?	*(Is) Abdel Aziz there* (lit. *present*)?
áywa, húwwa mawjúud.	*Yes, he (is) here.*
fáaTimah mawjúud-ah?	*(Is) Fatimah there?*
laa, híyya muu mawjúud-ah.	*No, she is not here.*

TIP

The word **muu** is used to make a noun or adjective negative.

Hiwaar 2 *Conversation 2*

02.08 *Mohammed wants to get in touch with Alex later.*

Mohammed	yaa áliks, kam rágam tilifóon-ak, min fáDHlak?
Alex	dagíigah … rágam tilifóon-i khámsah, Sifr, tís:ah, síttah, thaláathah, wáaHid.
Mohammed	shúkran, yaa áliks.
Alex	áfwan. wa rágam tilifóon-ak ínta?
Mohammed	rágam tilifóon-i khámsah, ithnáin, wáaHid, sáb:ah, Sifr, thamáanyah.
Alex	shwáyya, shwáyya! márrah tháaniyah, min fáDHlak!
Mohammed	zain. khámsah … ithnáin … wáaHid … sáb:ah … Sifr … thamáanyah.
Alex	shúkran, yaa muHámmad.
Mohammed	:áfwan.

RÁGAM TILIFÓON-AK ÍNTA YOUR TELEPHONE NUMBER

Although it is clear from the suffix **-ak** that the speaker is saying *your telephone number*, the added **ínta** emphasizes *your*.

1 **Find the phrases Alex and Mohammed use for the following:**

   a What's your telephone number?

   b My telephone number is ...

2 **Are these statements true (T) or false (F)?**

   a Alex asks for Mohammed's phone number.

   b Alex's phone number is 509631.

   c Mohammed's number is 521408.

> **TIP**
> Telephone numbers in spoken Arabic are given in a straight series of digits, e.g. 123 456 – just like English.

PRACTICE 2

1 **Rearrange the following numbers in ascending order.**

   a síttah

   c khámsah

   e wáaHid

   b thaláathah

   d ithnáin

   f árba:ah

2 02.09 **Listen to some of these Arabic numbers being read out in random order. Which numbers do you hear?**

   9   2   6   4   3   10   0   1   7   5

3 02.10 **Listen to these words then say them out loud after the speakers. Note the difference in sound between the similar letters, such as S and s, T and t.**

   a Sifr   sáb:ah

   b briTáaniya   al-imaráat

   c faránsa   miSr

   d ayrlánda   min fáDHlak

> **PRONUNCIATION TIP**
> Some Arabic words have capital letters in their transliteration. Why? These are different letters from non-capitalized ones. When you pronounce these, hollow your tongue down in your mouth to get the right sound.

4 **Do you remember what these words mean? Say what they are in English.**

5 02.11 **Listen to the speakers, then note what nationality each person is.**

   a _____

   b _____

   c _____

   d _____

   e _____

   f _____

2 ta-takállam :árabi? Do you speak Arabic?   **25**

6 02.12 **Read what each person says about themselves and match them with their nationality.**

1 ísm-i saif wa ána min :umaan
2 ísm-i fáadiya, ána yamaníyyah
3 ána nuur wa ána min al-imaaráat
4 ísm-i sáwsan. ána sauudiyyah
5 ána ísm-i Hamdáan, wa ána min al-iráaq
6 ísm-i muHámmad. ána gátari

a Yemen   b Saudi Arabia
c Iraq   d Qatar
e Emirates   f Oman

Go further

 READING ARABIC

Originally, the ancient Arabic language was written with far fewer letters, many of which had several different pronunciations. To prevent confusion, dots were added to these letters to distinguish between the various pronunciations. In Modern Arabic, the 'dot system' uses the following combinations:

▶ one, two or three letters above the letter.
▶ one or two (but not three) dots below the letter.

Many letters have no dots at all.

In this unit you will learn five letters which form the largest group: **b** (**baa'**), **t** (**taa'**), **th** (**thaa'**), **n** (**nuun**) and **y** (**yaa'**). They are identical, apart from the number and placement of the dots and the variations in the final and separate forms of two of them **n** and **y**. All are small in height, and all join both preceding and following letters.

end of a word	middle of a word	start of a word	on its own
كتب kútub *books*	سبعة sáb:ah *seven*	بحر báHar *sea*	ب baa'
الكويت al-kuwáit *Kuwait*	كتاب kitáab *book*	تسعة tísa:ah *nine*	ت taa'
ثالث tháalith *third*	كثير kathíir *much*	ثلاثة thaláathah *three*	ث thaa'
من min *from*	بنك bank *bank*	نور nuur *light*	ن nuun
عربي :árabi *Arab/Arabic*	جنسية jinsíyyah *nationality*	يد yad *hand*	ي yaa'

1 Match each Arabic letter to its English sound.

a ي   **1** nuun
b ت   **2** thaa'
c ن   **3** yaa'
d ث   **4** baa'
e ب   **5** taa'

2 Look at the Arabic words and match them to their transliteration.

> **TIP**
> In each work, look for the letters you have learned in the first two units, and use the alphabet chart in the Introduction if you need more help.

	Arabic		Transliteration
a	أنا	1	lándan
b	لندن	2	min
c	دبي	3	al-baHráin
d	من	4	ána
e	البحرين	5	dubáy

Test yourself

 1 Say these nationalities in Arabic:
  a English (m)   d Kuwaiti (f)
  b French (f)   e Scottish (m)
  c Qatari (m)   f Bahraini (f)

 2 Say these numbers in Arabic:
  a 7   e 6
  b 3   f 2
  c 9   g 5
  d 1   h 10

3 How do you say these phone numbers in Arabic?
  a 055 284 3134
  b 06 183 7499
  c 04 751 6281

SELF CHECK

I CAN...

- ... state my nationality.
- ... say what languages I speak.
- ... count from 0 to 10 in Arabic.
- ... ask for and give telephone numbers.
- ... ask for someone on the telephone.

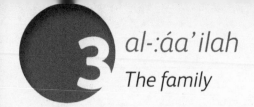

3 al-:áa'ilah

The family

In this unit you will learn how to:
▶ *say where you live.*
▶ *talk about people's occupations.*
▶ *talk about your family.*
▶ *talk about more than one person.*

CEFR: (A1) *Can ask and answer questions about themselves and other people, where they live and what they do for a living; can describe his or her family.*

Getting to know Arabs

Arabs are famous for their hospitality. Although some Gulf cities such as Dubai can seem to be dominated by expatriates, away from big cities you will not find it difficult to meet local people. Getting to know them may involve an invitation to drink **gáhwah** (*coffee*), eat dates and meet the extended family. This could include **al-wáalid** or **al-ab** (*the father*), **al-wáalidah** or **al-umm** (*the mother*) and **al-awláad** (*the children*), but perhaps also **al-akh** (*the brother*) or **al-ukht** (*the sister*).

Arabs are interested in strangers and will casually ask personal questions such as **aish ti-shtághal?** (*What do you do for a living?*), or **kam wálad :índ-ak?** to a man or **kam wálad :índ-ich?** to a woman (*How many children (lit. child) do you have?*). If you arrive alone, a common question is **wain al-awláad?** (*Where are the children?*). But do not take offence at this. Arabs take great pleasure in their children and will often show surprise to learn that Westerners have none or perhaps only one or two children. Sharing information about each other's work and families is part of getting to know people and of eventually becoming **aSdigáa'** (*friends*), a concept taken very seriously in Arab society.

 You may be offered **gáhwah** or **shaay** to drink. What do these words mean?

Vocabulary builder

OCCUPATIONS

 03.01 Listen to these occupations and repeat out loud, trying to imitate the speakers' pronunciation.

al-máhan	*occupations*
Tabíib	*doctor* (male)
Tabíibah	*doctor* (female)
muhándis	*engineer* (male)
muhándisah	*engineer* (female)
mumárriDH	*nurse* (male)
mumárriDHah	*nurse* (female)
mudárris	*teacher* (male)
mudárrisah	*teacher* (femaie)
Táalib	*student* (male)
Táalibah	*student* (female)
mudíir shárikah	*company director* (male)
mudíirat shárikah	*company director* (female)

> **TIP**
> Words for occupations have different masculine and feminine forms, with an **-ah** sound added to form the feminine.

FAMILY MEMBERS

 03.02 First add the missing words, then listen and try to imitate the speakers.

al-:áa'ilah	*the family*
zooj	*husband*
zóojah	*wife*
wálad (awláad)	*boy/son* (*boys/sons* – pl)
	(can also mean *children*)
bint (banáat)	*girl/daughter* (_____/_____)
ab or **wáalid**	*father*
umm or **wáalidah**	*mother*
akh (ikhwáan)	*brother* (*brothers*)
ukht (akhawáat)	*sister* (_____)

NEW EXPRESSIONS

03.03 **wain tí-skun?** — *Where do you live?* (to a man)

wain tí-skun-íin? — *Where do you live?* (to a _____)

al-Hiin — *now*

á-skun fii ... — *I live in ...*

aish ti-shtághal? — *What do you do* (lit. *work*)? (to a man)

aish ti-shtaghal-íin? — *What do you do* (lit. *work*)? (to a (_____)

ána mumárriDH — *I'm a nurse* (masculine)

ána mumárriDHah — *I'm a nurse* (feminine)

maa a-shtághal — *I don't work*

a-shtághal fii ... — *I (_____) in ...*

mádrasah — *a school*

mustáshfa — *a hospital*

bank — *a bank*

shárikah — *a company*

máktab — *an office*

kabíir — *big* (masculine)

kabíirah — *big* (feminine)

láakin — *but*

al-Hiin dáwr-ak! *Now your turn!*

Cofi is a teacher. How would he say in Arabic where he works?

 # Hiwaar 1 *Conversation 1*

03.04 *Rahma and Sally are talking about where they live, and what they and their husbands do for a living. Listen while you follow the text, then answer the questions.*

1 Where does Sally live? Does she work?

Rahma	wain ti-skun-íin al-Hiin ya sáali?
Sally	á-skun fii dubáy. wa íntu wain ti-skun-úun?
Rahma	ná-skun fii másqaT láakin níHna min Suur.
Sally	w ínti aish ti-shtaghal-íin?
Rahma	ána mumárriDHah - a-shtághal fii mustáshfa. w ínti?
Sally	ána maa a-shtághal al-Hiin láakin zóoj-i muhándis, yi-shtághal fii shárikah kabíirah fii ábu DHábi. wa zooj-ich, aish yi-shtághal?
Rahma	yi-shtághal al-Hiin fii bank.
Sally	maa shaa' Al-láah.

32

2 Read the text again, then answer the questions.
  a What does Rahma do for a living?
  b Where does Sally's husband work?
  c Where does Rahma's husband work?

3 What are these phrases in Arabic? Say your answers out loud.
  a Where do you live now? (f)   **d** What do you do? (f)
  b We live in Muscat.   **e** I'm a nurse.
  c ... but we are from Sur.   **f** I don't work.

Language discovery

1 What Arabic word is used in the conversation for *we* **and** *you* **(plural)?**

2 What do these three forms of the verb *to work* **mean?**

Example: a *a-shtághal I work*
  a *a-shtághal*   **b** *ti-shtaghal-íin*   **c** *yi-shtághal*

PLURAL PRONOUNS

In Arabic the pronouns used for *we*, *you* (plural) and *they* are the same, whether you are talking about males or females.

níHna	*we*
íntu	*you*
húmma	*they*

PRESENT TENSE VERBS

To form the present tense in Arabic you need a present stem (the 'core' of the verb), a prefix (letters before the stem) and in some cases a suffix (letters after the stem). In Arabic, the present stem of the verb *to live* is **skun**.

Arabic – singular	English	Arabic – plural	English
(ána) á-skun	I live	(níHna) ná-skun	we live
(inta) tí-skun	you (m) live	(íntu) ti-skun-úun	you live (m/f)
(inti) ti-skun-íin	you (f) live		
(húwwa) yí-skun	he lives	(húmma) yi-skun-úun	they live (m/f)
(híyya) tí-skun	she lives		

Notes

1 Pronouns (ána, ínta, ínti, etc.) are not always used with verbs as the verb prefix and in some cases suffix tells us who or what the subject is. The verb forms for *you* (m) and *she* are identical, but it is the context that tells us who is the subject of the verb.

2 Many Gulf Arabs alter or omit the vowel of the prefixes yi- and ti-, so you may hear yu-, tu-, ya-, ta- or even y-, t-.

3 Some dialects omit the final -n in the endings -íin and -úun.

al-Hiin dáwr-ak! *Now your turn!*

Complete the verb work using the correct pronouns, prefixes, suffixes and English translations.

Arabic (singular)	English	Arabic (plural)	English
(ána) _____ -shtághal	_____ work	_____ na-shtághal	we work
(ínta) _____ -shtaghal	you (m) work	(íntu) ti-shtághal-úun	_____ (pl) work (m/f)
(ínti) ti-shtághal _____	you (f) work		
(húwwa) _____ -shtághal	he works	(húmma) _____ -shtaghal-úun	they work (m/f)
(híyya) ti-shtághal	_____ works		

> **TIP**
> In Arabic there is no word for the indefinite article, i.e. *a* or *an*. Instead, just use the noun on its own. For example:
> **ána Tabíib** I (am) (a) doctor (m)
> **a-shtághal fii mustáshfa** I work in (a) hospital

al-Hiin dáwr-ak! *Now your turn!*

How would you say *He works in a company*?

 PRACTICE 1

1 Choose the correct pronoun to complete each sentence.

   a níHna/húmma yi-skun-úun fii :ajmáan.
   b ínti/ínta ti-skun-íin wain?
   c níHna/ána a-shtághal fii gáTar al-Hiin.
   d íntu/níHna ti-shtaghal-úun wain?

34

2 Choose the correct form of the verb to work to complete each sentence.

a húwwa yi-shtághal/ti-shtághal fii bank.

b híyya ti-shtaghal-íin/ti-shtághal fii mustáshfa.

c ána a-shtághal/yi-shtághal fii sháarikah kabíirah.

d húmma na-shtághal/yi-shtaghal-úun fii dubáy.

3 Choose the correct word for each person's job, depending on whether the subject is masculine or feminine.

a híyya mudárris/mudárrisah. (She (is a) teacher.)

b húwwa Tabíibah/Tabíib. (He (is a) doctor.)

c sáalim (m) mikáaniki/mikaanikíyyah. (He (is a) mechanic.)

d fáaTimah (f) muhándisah/muhándis. (She (is an) engineer.)

4 Rearrange the order of the Arabic words below so that the sentence matches its English translation.

sháarikah a-shtághal wa muhándis ána fii

I am an engineer and I work in a company.

5 Answer these questions about yourself.

a wain tí-skun/ti-skun-íin? (Where do you live?)

b aish ti-shtághal/ti-shtaghal-íiin? (What do you do?)

c wain ti-shtághal/ti-shtaghal-íin? (Where do you work?)

6 Read what these people say about their work, then decide whether the person speaking is male (m) or female (f).

a ána muhándisah, ashtághal fii sháarikah.

b ashtághal fii mádrasah, ána mudárris.

c ána Tabíib, a-shtághal fii mustáshfa.

d ána maa a-shtághal, ána Táalibah.

e ána mudíirat sháarikah.

f ána mumárriDH, ashtághal fii mustáshfa.

7 Are these people talking about one person or more than one (singular or plural)?

a málik yí-skun fi l-baHráin.

b sáarah wa Táariq yi-skun-úun fii bait kabíir.

c ti-skun-úun fi d-dóoHah?

d jain tí-skun fi l-kuwáit.

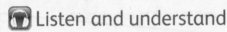 Listen and understand

1 03.05 **What do these people do for a living? Careful, there are two extra jobs you won't need!**

a :áli

b máriyam

c fáaris

d básma

e jamáal

f híbah

> student   company director   engineer
> nurse   teacher   doctor
> mechanic   bank manager

2 03.06 **Add the missing word to complete the English translation.**

a I am a _____.

b He works in a _____.

c My parents _____ in Bahrain.

d Do you _____ in Dubai?

e Where does he _____?

f She doesn't _____ in Al-Ain.

Hiwáar 2 *Conversation 2*

03.07 **First listen to Fatima and Sally talk about their families, then answer the questions.**

1 **How many children does Sally have? What are their ages?**

Fatima	:índ-ich awláad ya sáali?
Sally	áywa, :índi wálad wa bint.
Fatima	(*laughing*) bass?
Sally	(*laughing with her*) áywa, w ínti?
Fatima	níHna :índ-na síttah, thaláthah awláad wa thaláth banáat.
Sally	maa shaa' Al-láah!
Fatima	al-wálad kam :úmr-uh?
Sally	mm, al-wálad :úmr-uh tís:a wa l-bint :úmr-ha khámas sanawáat.

kam wálad :índ-ich? | *How many children do you (f) have? (can also mean How many boys/sons do you have?)*

(ána) :índ-i | *I have*

(níHna) :índ-na | *we have*

maa sháa' Al-láah | *Wow!*

al-awláad kam :úmr-hum? | *How old are your children?*

:úmr-uh khámas sanawáat | *he is 5 years old*

:úmr-ha thamáan sanawáat | *she is 8 years old*

> **TIP**
>
> **maa sháa' Alláah** is often used to express joy, appreciation or gratitude and literally means *God has willed it*. Often used to ward off jealousy or misfortune, it can be seen on cars, shop windows and even street signs as a reminder that all accomplishments are achieved by the will of God, including the journey home.

---

2 Listen to the conversation again, then answer these questions.

   a How many children does Sally have?

   b How many daughters does Fatima have?

   c How old is Sally's daughter?

 3 Can you say the Arabic for the following?

   a Do you (f) have any children?

   b Is that all?!

   c We have six.

Language discovery

 1 What is the Arabic for *three girls/daughters*?

2 If :úmr-i means *my age*, to what do the endings on the words :úmr-uh and :úmr-ha in the conversation refer?

PLURALS

Arabic plurals are often irregular so the best approach is to learn the plural together with the singular of a noun (shown in brackets in the Vocabulary builder).

wálad (*boy/son*)   **awláad** (*boys/sons*)

sánah (*year*)   **sanawáat** (*years*)

POSSESSIVE SUFFIXES

You have already learned the possessive suffix endings for *my* and *your*.
Here are the endings for *his, her, our* and *their*.

Arabic possessive suffix	English possessive pronoun
-uh	*his*
-ha	*her*
-na	*our*
-kum	*your* (plural m/f)
-hum	*their* (m/f)

:úmr-**uh** sitt sanawáat   *he is six years old* (lit. *life-his six years*)

bint-**ha** ísm-**ha** jamíilah   *her daughter is called Jamila*
                                         (lit. *daughter-her name-her Jamila*)

> **SITT OR SITTAH?**
> Arabic has both feminine and masculine forms of numbers, e.g. **sitt** (m) and **sittah** (f),
> and there are special rules as to when to use which. For further details, see *Complete
> Spoken Arabic* or *Complete Arabic* .

PRACTICE 2

1 **Add the correct plural form of these words. Refer to the
   Vocabulary builder at the start of the unit if you need help.**
   a bint (*girl*) _____ a akh (*brother*) _____ c ukht _____

2 **Complete each sentence by adding the correct word in each
   space.**
   a ʿínd-i thaláathah _____ (*boys*) wa thaláth _____ (*girls*).
   b bínt-i :úmr-ha khámas _____ (*years (old)*).
   c ʿínd-i árba: _____ (*sisters*).

3 **Choose the correct possessive suffix for the following:**
   a bínt-i :úmr(-uh/-ha) áab:a sanawáat.
   b ákh-i úmr(-uh/-ha) :sitt sanawáat.
   c al-awláad :úmr(-na/-hum) thaláth wa thamáan sanawáat.

Now translate each sentence into English.

Go further

 READING ARABIC

The group of letters **j** (**jiim**), **H** (**Haa'**) and **kh** (**khaa'**) all have the same basic shape and are distinguished only by dots. Remember to refer to the pronunciation guide when practising the sound of these letters.

j or ج has a dot below the basic shape.

H or ح has no dot at all.

kh or خ has a dot above the basic shape.

In handwriting, including calligraphy on street shop and signs, the joining strokes from the previous letters are often looped over the top like this:

end of a word	middle of a word	start of a word	alone
الخليج **al-khalíij** *the Gulf*	عجمان **:ajmáan** *Ajman (an Emirate)*	جدة **jáddah** *grandmother*	ج **jiim**
صالح **SáaliH** *Salih (a male's name)*	البحرين **al-baHráin** *Bahrain (a country)*	حمد **Hámad** *Hamad (a male's name)*	ح **Haa'**
شيخ **shaikh** *sheikh (ruler)*	أخت **ukht** *sister*	خالد *Khalid (a male's name)*	خ **khaa'**

 TIP

The second letter in this group, **H**, is very common in the numerous personal names which derive from the root **H-m-d** meaning *praise* e.g. **muHámmad**, **Hámad**, **maHmúud** and **áHmad**.

Match the Arabic writing to its correct transliteration in Arabic. For help, look out for the letters in their different positions (beginning, middle and end of word).

	Arabic		Transliteration
a	جنوب	1	Hámad (name)
b	زوجة	2	al-baHráin (Bahrain)
c	حمد	3	khaTT (script)
d	أخت	4	akh (brother)
e	الخليج	5	janúub (south)
f	أخ	6	zóojah (wife)
g	البحرين	7	al-khalíij (the Gulf)
h	خط	8	ukht (sister)

 Test yourself

Read the email Fatima writes to introduce herself and her family, then answer the question.

1 Can you guess the meaning of **rábbat al-bait**?

ána ísm-i fáaTimah wa á-skun fii nizwa fii :umáan. :úmr-i :ishríin sánah. abú-i ísm-uh kháalid. húwwa muhándis wa yi-shtághal fii shárikah kabíirah fii nízwa. úmm-i maa ti-shtághal, híyya rábbat al-bait. :índi thaláathah ikhwáan wa húmma yi-shtaghal-úun fii másqaT.

TIP	
bait	house
:ashríin	twenty
abú-i	my father

2 Answer these questions to check your understanding.

   a Where does Fatima live?

   b How old is she?

   c What does Fatima's father do?

   d How many brothers does Fatima have?

3 Choose the correct word to complete each sentence.

   a ána :úmr-i/:úmr-uh thalaathíin sánah.

   b ínti ti-shtághal/ti-shtaghal-íin wain?

   c al-wálad kam :úmr-uh/:úmr-ha?

   d bint-i yí-skun/tí-skun fii jáddah.

   e abú-i maa yi-shtághal/ti-shtághal al-Hiin.

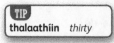

TIP
thalaathíin *thirty*

4 Use what you have learned in this unit to answer these questions about yourself. Speak your answers out loud.

   a wain tí-skun/ti-skun-íin?

   b aish ti-shtághal/ti-shtaghal-íin?

   c :índ-ak/:índ-ich awláad/ikhwáan/akhawáat?

SELF CHECK

	I CAN. . .
⦿	... say where I live.
⦿	... talk about people's occupations.
⦿	... talk about my family.
⦿	... talk about more than one person.

Review: Units 1–3

 1 You have just met Mohammed at the conference banquet at 7p.m. Greet him out loud with the correct Arabic phrase.

    a SabáaH al-khair   **c** masáa' al-khair

    b má:a as-saláamah   **d** al-Hámdu li-l-láah bi-kháir

 2 Match the Arabic to the English, saying the Arabic out loud.

    a ána ísm-i …   **1** I'm fine thanks.

    b kaif Háal-ak?   **2** What do you do?

    c al-Hámdu li-l-láah bi-kháir.   **3** I'm from London.

    d ána min lándan.   **4** Goodbye.

    e ta-takállam inglíizi?   **5** My name is…

    f aish ti-shtághal?   **6** Do you speak English?

    g má:a as-saláamah.   **7** How are you?

3 There are two words for you (singular) in Arabic – ínta or ínti. Which would you use for the following people?

    a your sister   **c** your friend's brother

    b your male boss   **d** the female receptionist

4 Match the English to the correct possessive endings in Arabic.

    a my   **1** -ak

    b your (m)   **2** -ha

    c your (f)   **3** -i

    d his   **4** -ich/-ish/-ik

    e her   **5** -uh

 5 You want to know a little more about Mohammed. Match each question to its correct translation, then speak the Arabic out loud.

    a Where do you come from?   **1** ta-takállam inglíizi?

    b Where do you live?   **2** aish ti-shtághal?

    c What do you do?   **3** :ind-ak awláad?

    d Do you speak English?   **4** wain tí-skun?

    e Do you have children?   **5** ínta min wain?

6 Give the feminine form for each of these words.

   a ána inglíiz-i   _____

   b ána gáTar-i   _____

   c ána Tabíib   _____

   d ána mudárris   _____

   e ána amríik-i   _____

7 What does each phrase in the previous exercise mean in English?

8 Match the number words in transliterated Arabic to the correct English and Arabic numerals.

   a ithnáin   **1**   ه

   b :áshara   **7**   ٨

   c khámsah   **3**   ١

   d thaláathah   **8**   ٢

   e sáb:ah   **2**   ١٠

   f wáaHid   **5**   ٣

   g thamáanyah   **10**   ٧

9 You have just met an Arab who asks you the following questions. Answer each question out loud in Arabic, giving information about yourself. Try to speak with good pronunciation!

   a aish ísm-ak/ísm-ich?

   b ínta/ínti min wain?

   c wain tí-skun/ti-skun-íin?

   d ta-takállam :árabi?

   e kam rágam tilifóon-ak?

   f wain ti-shtághal/ti-shtaghal-íin al-Hiin?

   g :índ-ak/:índ-ich awláad?

10 This sign says 'Now open'. Which Arabic word means maftúuH (*open*)?

   a the top word

   b the bottom word?

11 **The Arabic word for** *post* **is baríid and the Arabic for** *office* **is máktab.**

    a Which of the Arabic words in the sign says **baríid**: the first or the second?

    b Which word has **al** (*the*) in front of it, **baríid** or **máktab**?

Try to identify the letters you have learned in Units 1 to 3.

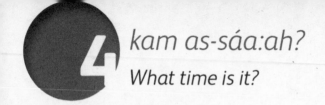

kam as-sáa:ah?

What time is it?

In this unit you will learn how to:
▶ *ask for and tell the time.*
▶ *ask when places open or close.*
▶ *talk about days of the week.*
▶ *talk about different times of day.*

CEFR: (A1) *Can indicate time by such phrases as 'three o'clock' and can communicate in simple and routine tasks requiring a simple and direct exchange of information.*

Hours of the day

The working day in the Gulf starts between **as-sáa:ah sába:ah** (*seven o'clock*) and **as-sáa:ah thamáanyah** (*eight o'clock*) in the morning and for many workers ends between one and two **bá:d aDH-Dhuhr** (*in the afternoon*). Were you to visit a ministry or other government department at 3 p.m., you would probably find it **magfúul** (*closed*) for the day, but the **suug** (*market*) and smaller businesses such as tailors open again in the early afternoon when temperatures are cooler. Open again in the evening when temperatures are cooler. This is when families go shopping together, and you will often see groups of women haggling with the **khayyáaT** (*tailor*) over the price and completion date of a custom-made dress, people buying their food for the week, and others just enjoying the chance to get out for a walk.

Visitors to the region are often surprised to learn that the weekend in most Gulf countries falls on **yoom al-júma:ah** (*Friday*) and **yoom as-sabt** (*Saturday*). **al-júma:ah** is the Muslim day of prayer and in most parts of the Gulf offices and businesses are closed all day on Friday and Saturday. However, for the **suug**, the mall and other smaller shops, it is a seven-day week wherever you are.

> **PRONUNCIATION TIP**
> The word **yoom** is often omitted, especially with **al-júma:ah**.

If **yoom ath-thaláathah** (*Tuesday*) means *the third day*, can you work out which numbers these days of the week correspond to? **al-ithnáin, al-árba:ah, al-khamíis**

Vocabulary builder

TIMES OF THE DAY

04.01 **Add the missing words, then listen and try to imitate the pronunciation of the speakers.**

aS-Súb(a)H	(the) morning
aDH-DHúh(u)r	(the) noon
bá:d aDH-Dhúh(u)r	afternoon (lit. after the-noon)
al-mása	(the) evening
al-lail	(the) night
as-sáa:ah sáb:ah aS-Súb(a)H	7 a.m.
as-sáa:ah tís:ah fi l-lail	9 _____

NEW EXPRESSIONS

04.02 | kam as-sáa:ah? | What time is it? |
|---|---|
| as-sáa:ah thaláathah | it's _____ o'clock |
| bi DH-DHabt | exactly |
| wa nuSS | half past |
| fiih maT:am hína fi l-fúndug (funduq)? | Is there a restaurant here in the hotel? |
| fiih ... | There is ... |
| máT:am | (a) restaurant |
| másbaH | (a) pool |
| yí-ftaH | it opens (m) |
| tí-ftaH | it opens (f) |
| yi-bánnid | it closes (m) |
| ti-bánnid | it closes (f) |
| yí-ftaH as-sáa:ah kam? | What time does it (m) _____? |
| tí-ftaH as-sáa:ah kam? | What time does it (f) _____? |
| fi l-lail | in the evening |
| maftúuH | open (m) |
| maftúuHah | open (f) |
| magfúul (maqfúul) | closed (m) |
| magfúulah(maqfúulah) | _____ (f) |
| tagríiban (taqríiban) | approximately, around |

aw	*or*
ashkúr-ak	*(I) thank you* (to a man)
ashkúr-_____	*(I) thank you* (to a woman)
áhlan wa sáhlan	*hello, also (you're) welcome*

> **TIP**
> You may hear the local words **mbánnad** (*closed*) and **mbáTTal** (*open*) but as these can't be used in all contexts, it's best to stick to **maftúuH** and **magfúul**.

🎧 Hiwaar 1 *Conversation 1*

04.03 *Peter has just arrived at a hotel in Muscat after a night flight from London. He asks the receptionist about the local time as his watch is showing 3 a.m. (London time). First listen, then answer the question.*

1   What is the time difference between London and Muscat?

Peter	yaa akhú-i, kam as-sáa:ah?
káatib	al-Hiin as-sáa:ah sáb:ah.
Peter	as-sáa:ah sáb:ah bi DH-DHábt?
káatib	ná:am, bi DH-DHábt.
Peter	shúkran.
káatib	:áfwan.
Peter	fiih máT:am híni fi l-fúndug?
káatib	ná:am, fiih. …láakin húwwa magfúul al-Hiin.
Peter	as-sáa:ah kam yí-ftaH?
káatib	yí-ftaH as-sáa:ah sáb:ah wa nuSS, yá:ani … ba:d nuSS sáa:ah.
Peter	ashkúr-ak.
káatib	áhlan wa sáhlan.

> **TIP**
> **káatib**   *receptionist* (m)
> **híni**   *variation of* **hína** (*here*)

> **TIP**
> **akhú-i**, literally meaning *my brother*, is a friendly term often used to address a man, even if you don't know him. Similarly, you can use the term **úkht-i**, *my sister*, for a woman.

Peter	wa fiih másbaH?
káatib	áiwa fiih.
Peter	as-sáa:ah kam yi-bánnid fi l-lail?
káatib	yá:ani ... as-sáa:ah síttah aw sába:ah tagríiban.
Peter	shúkran.
káatib	:áfwan.

TIP

The term **yá:ani** has various meanings such as *well, hmm, kind of, sort of.* You will hear it a lot and in order to sound really authentic you should start using it right away!

2 When does the restaurant open?

3 How long must Peter wait before he can get something to eat at the restaurant?

4 What two things does he ask about the pool?

Language discovery

1 Find the phrase which means *seven o'clock.*

2 Find the phrase which means *It is closed now.*

TELLING THE TIME

04.05 To say *o'clock* in Arabic just say **as-sáa:ah** plus a number. It can mean both *it is … o'clock* and *at … o'clock.*

kam as-sáa:ah?	*What time is it?*
as-sáa:ah wáaH(i)dah	*one o'clock*
as-sáa:ah thintáin	*two o'clock*
as-sáa:ah thaláathah	*three o'clock*
as-sáa:ah árba:ah	*four o'clock*
as-sáa:ah khámsah	*five o'clock*
as-sáa:ah síttah	*six o'clock*
as-sáa:ah sába:ah	*seven o'clock*
as-sáa:ah thamáanyah	*eight o'clock*
as-sáa:ah tís:ah	*nine o'clock*

as-sáa:ah :ásharah	*ten o'clock*
as-sáa:ah (iHdá:shar)	*eleven o'clock*
as-sáa:ah (ithná:shar)	*twelve o'clock*
wa khams	*five past*
wa rúba:	*quarter past*
wa thilth	*twenty past* (lit. *and a third (of an hour)*)
wa nuSS	*half past*
ílla thilth	*twenty to* (lit. *less a third (of an hour)*)
ílla rúba:	*a quarter to* (lit. *less a quarter*)
ílla khams	*five to* (lit. *less five*)

In English you say *past*, but in Arabic you say **wa** (*and* or *plus*):
as-sáa:ah wáaHdah wa rúba: lit. *the hour is one plus a quarter (quarter past one)*

Twenty-five past and *twenty-five to* the hour are expressed in Arabic as *the hour plus a half minus five*, and *the hour plus a half plus five* respectively.

as-sáa:ah khámsah wa-nuSS ílla khams	*twenty-five past five*
as-sáa:ah khámsah wa-nuSS wa khams	*twenty-five to six*

GENDER OF NOUNS

In Arabic, nouns are either masculine or feminine in gender. So when you want to ask when somewhere is open or closed, you need to know if the place is masculine or feminine so you can use the correct verb form or adjective. In English we would say *it* but in Arabic you use **húwwa** (*he*) and **híyya** (*she*) for non-human nouns.

húwwa magfúul	lit. *he is closed*
híyya magfúulah	lit. *she is closed*

Equally, you must use either the masculine or feminine verb form according to the gender of the noun.

al-máT:am yí-ftaH   *the restaurant opens*
(**máT:am** is masculine)

aS-Saydalíyyah tí-ftaH   *the pharmacy opens*
(**Saydalíyyah** is feminine)

As a general rule, most nouns ending in **-ah** are feminine but there are exceptions such as **umm** (*mother*) and **bint** (*girl*), which are both feminine.

PRACTICE 1

1 Match the correct time to each statement.

a	as-sáa:ah árba:ah wa rúb:a:	3:45/4:15
b	as-sáa:ah khámsah ílla thilth	4:40/5:20
c	as-sáa:ah thamáanyah wa nuSS	8:30/9:30
d	as-sáa:ah iHdá:shar wa khams	10:55/11:05
e	as-sáa:ah thintáin wa nuSS ílla khams	2:25/2:35

 2 First ask what the time is, then say the time shown on each clock face.

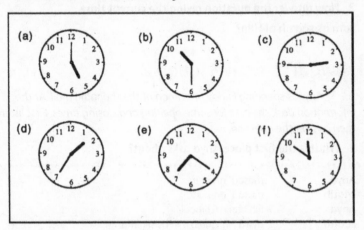

3 Select the correct word for *open* and *closed* according to the gender of each noun as given.

a	as-suug (m)	maftúH/maftúHah
b	as-síinima (f)	maftúH/maftúHah
c	al-bank (m)	magfúul/magfúulah
d	al-baríid (m)	maftúH/maftúHah
e	al-mustáshfa (f)	magfúul/magfúulah

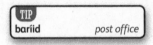

TIP

baríid   *post office*

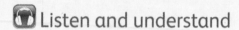 Listen and understand

1 04.06 **Listen, then select the correct time for each statement.**

a 7:00/8:00/9:00   d 2:15/3:15/3:45

b 9:30/11:30/3:30   e 6:50/7:10/7:50

c 4:05/4:25/4:35   f 11:55/12:05/12:55

 2 04.06 **Listen again and repeat the times. Take care to pronounce the :ain in sáa:ah correctly.**

3 **Now answer the question giving the current time.**

kam as-sáa:ah al-Hiin?

 Hiwáar 2 *Conversation 2*

04.07 *Anya is spending Friday afternoon at the shopping mall. At the information desk she asks for some opening and closing times. First listen, then answer the question.*

1 **What is the first place Anya asks about?**

Anya	masáa' al khair.
káatib	masáa' an-nuur.
Anya	fiih baríid fi l-mool?
káatib	aywa fiih, garíib min as-síinima.
Anya	húwwa maftúuH al-Hiin?
káatib	laa, húwwa magfúul yoom al-júma:ah.
Anya	Táb:an! aS-Saydalíyyah magfúulah ba:d?
káatib	laa, híyya maftúHah.
Anya	as-sáa:ah kam ti-bánnid?
káatib	ti-bánnid as-sáa:ah khámsah.
Anya	w as-síinima, as-sáa:ah kam tí-ftaH fi l-lail?
káatib	as-síinima maftúHah Tool al-yoom kull yoom! ti-bánnid as-sáa:ah ithná:shar fi l-lail.
Anya	shúkran jazíilan.
káatib	:áfwan.

TIP	
ba:d	*also, too* (also *still* and *after* depending on context)
Tool al-yoom	*all day*
kull* yoom	*every day*
***kull** is often pronounced **kill** in the Gulf	

2 What is the problem with the first place Anya would like to visit?

3 Is the pharmacy open right now?

4 When is the cinema open?

5 04.07 Listen again and speak the part of Anya. You begin.

Language discovery

1 Can you find the phrase in the conversation that means
   It is closed on Friday?

ayáam al-usbúu *days of the week*

yoom al-áHad	*Sunday*
yoom al-ithnáin	*Monday*
yoom ath-thaláathah	*Tuesday*
yoom al-árba:ah	*Wednesday*
yoom al-khamíis	*Thursday*
yoom al-júma:ah	*Friday*
yoom as-sabt	*Saturday*

2 As the next day starts from sundown in Islam, sunset on
   Saturday is the beginning of Sunday. So, if you receive an
   invitation to a wedding on **láilat al-áHad** (lit. *night of Sunday*),
   when should you turn up?

   a Sunday evening   b Sunday morning   c Saturday evening

3 What does **ti-bánnid as-sáa:ah ithná:ashar fi l-lail** mean?

Now that you know how to tell the time, say the days of the week and
times of the day, you can begin to make longer sentences, giving more
information.

<u>**al-bank**</u> **yi-ftaH as-sáa:ah kam yoom** <u>**al-áHad aS-Súbah**</u>?

What time does the bank open on Sunday morning?

<u>**al-mool**</u> **yi-bánnid as-sáa:ah kam yoom** <u>**al-khamíis fi l-lail**</u>?

What time does the mall close on Thursday evening?

al-Hiin dáwr-ak! *Now your turn!*

Using the examples as a guide, translate these questions into Arabic, changing the underlined words to say the following instead.

    a What time does the <u>pool</u> (m) open on <u>Wednesday morning</u>?

    b What time does the <u>restaurant</u> (m) close on <u>Saturday evening</u>?

  PRACTICE 2

1 When do these places open or close? Say the question then the answer, being sure to include the correct time of day.

Example: a bank opens? at 8 a.m.

al-bank yí-ftaH as-sáa:ah kam?

yí-ftaH as-sáa:ah thamáanyah aS-SúbaH.

    a bank (m) opens?   at 8 a.m.

    b mall (m) opens?   at 9 a.m.

    c cinema (f) closes?   at 11.30 p.m.

    d police station (m) opens?   at 7.15 a.m.

    e shop (m) closes?   at 1.30 p.m.

TIP			
al-bank	*the bank*	márkaz ash-shúrTah	*police station*
al-mool	*the mall*	ad-dukkáan	*the shop*

2 Read these times and write them out in English.

    a ١١:٣٠   **d** ١٢:١٥

    b ٩:١٠   **e** ١٥:٠٠

    c ٧:٢٥   **f** ٢٣:٥٥

3 Can you identify the business hours from morning to evening?

وقت العمل

٧ صباحـــاً

الى

١١ مســـاء

Go further

READING ARABIC

In this unit you will learn the letters **d** د and **dh** ذ (called **daal** and **dhaal**). **daal** and **dhaal** are two of the six letters that don't join onto the letter that follows them, as you can see in the table.

end of a word	middle of a word	start of a word	on its own
ولد **wálad** *boy*	صيدلية **Saydalíyyah** *pharmacy*	دكان **dukkáan** *shop*	د **daal**
خذ **khudh** *take*	هذا **háadha** *this* (masc)	ذلك **dháalik** *that*	ذ **dhaal**

1 Find the letter (daal) or (dhaal) in the following table. Do these letters appear at the beginning (B), middle (M) or end of each word (E)?

	Transliteration and meaning	Arabic word	Letter position
a	**awláad** *boys*	أولاد	B M E
b	**dubáy** *Dubai*	دبي	B M E
c	**baghdáad** *Baghdad*	بغداد	B M E
d	**jáddah** *grandmother*	جدة	B M E
e	**háadha** *this (m)*	هذا	B M E
f	**dukkáan** *shop*	دكان	B M E
g	**ad-dóoHah** *Doha*	الدوحة	B M E
	al-áHad *Sunday*	الأحد	B M E

2 Now highlight the letters daal and/or dhaal in each word.

Test yourself

 1 Say these times in Arabic, including the time of day.

Example: a 8 a.m. **as-sáa:ah thamáanyah aS-SúbaH**

a	8 a.m.	**e**	9.45 a.m.
b	2.30 p.m.	**f**	5.15 p.m.
c	6.10 p.m.	**g**	7.30 a.m.
d	4 p.m.	**h**	11.20 p.m.

2 How do you say these days of the week in Arabic?

a	Tuesday	**d**	Friday
b	Saturday	**e**	Monday
c	Thursday	**f**	Sunday

SELF CHECK

I CAN...

○ ... ask for and tell the time.

○ ... ask when places open or close.

○ ... talk about the days of the week.

○ ... talk about different times of day.

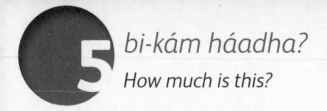

5 bi-kám háadha?

How much is this?

In this unit you will learn how to:
▶ *ask for an item in a shop.*
▶ *ask for something different.*
▶ *say what colour something is.*
▶ *recognize and use numbers 11–1 million.*
▶ *ask about prices.*

CEFR: (A2) *Can ask about things and make simple transactions in shops.*

🔘 Shopping

Shopping in the Gulf is an exhilarating experience, whether you seek top-end designer goods in a modern, air-conditioned **márkaz tijáari** or **mool** (*shopping centre* or *mall*), or prefer to barter for something more traditional in the bustling **suug**, where you will find all sorts of wonderful and exotic items. You may be tempted to buy a **míjmar** (*incense burner*), some **lubáan** (*frankincense*), or even a **khánjar** (*decorative dagger*). Haggling over prices in the **suug** is fun and a great way to escape the heat of the midday sun. At the glittering **suug adh-dh* áhab** (*gold market*)

you can buy and sell, trading in your **kháaTim gadíim** (*old ring*) or your **silsílah gadíimah** (*old necklace*) for the latest design at today's gold price. Whatever you are shopping for, you will need to know phrases such as **ti-sáwwi takhfiiDH?** (*Will you give me a discount?*) and **bikám áakhir?** (*What's your last price?*)

 In a souvenir shop you hear someone ask **al-khánjar bikám?** What does this mean in English?

Vocabulary builder

 05.01 Listen, then repeat the words and phrases out loud and try to imitate the speaker's pronunciation.

fi s-suug (suuq)	*at the market*
míjmar (m)	*incense burner*
bakhúur (m)	*spice incense mix*
lubáan (m)	*frankincense*
finjáan (m)	*(coffee) cup*
gamíiS/qamíiS (m)	*shirt*
fustáan (m)	*dress*
bantalóon (m)	*trousers*
kháaTim (m)	*ring*
silsílah (f)	*necklace*
buTáagah/buTáaqah (f)	*postcard*
zoolíyyah (f)	*carpet*

ADJECTIVES

kabíir/kabíirah	*big (m/f)*
Saghíir/Saghíirah	*small (m/f)*
Tawíil/Tawíilah	*long/tall (m/f)*
gaSíir/gaSíirah	*short (m/f)*
gháali/gháaliyah	*expensive (m/f)*
rakhíiS/rakhíiSah	*cheap (m/f)*
jamíil/jamíilah	*beautiful (m/f)*
jadíid/jadíidah	*new (m/f)*
gadíim/gadíimah (qadíim)	*old (m/f)*

 NEW EXPRESSIONS

05.02

aish tiríid/tirid-íin?	*What do you want? (to a man/woman)*
a-ríid a-shúuf	*I want to look (lit. I-want I-look)*
a-ríid a-shtári	*I want to buy … (lit. I-want I-buy)*
tfáDHDHal	*here you are (to a man)*
tfáDHDHali	*here you are (to a woman)*
húwwa gadíim?	*Is it old? (m) (lit. Is he old?)*
híyya gadíimah?	*Is it old? (f) (lit. Is she old?)*
fiih :índ-ak/-ich …?	*Do you (m/f) have …? (lit. Is there with you …?)*

tháani/tháaniyah	*another one* (m/f)
ákbar shwáyya	*a little bigger*
Táb:an	*of course*
wáajid, also **jíddan**	*very*

🎧 Hiwaar 1 *Conversation 1*

05.03 *Ali is at the* **suug,** *hoping to find something to take home to his family. First listen, then answer the question.*

1 What is the first item Ali looks at?

Ali	as-saláamu :aláikum.
SáaHib ad-dukkáan	w :aláikum as-saláam. aish ti-ríid?
Ali	a-ríid a-shúuf bass.
Ali looks around the shop for a while.	
Ali	a-ríid a-shtári míjmar.
SáaHib ad-dukkáan	*(hands one to him)* tfáDHDHal.
Ali	*(peering at it)* húwwa gadíim?
SáaHib ad-dukkáan	laa laa, húwwa jadíid. *(hands him another)* háadha wáajid gadíim.
Ali	shúkran. fiih :índ-ak tháani ákbar shwáyya?
SáaHib ad-dukkáan	Táb:an.
Ali looks around the shop a little more.	
Ali	wa az-zoolíyyah aS-Saghíirah jadíidah?
SáaHib ad-dukkáan	háadhi? áywa, híyya jadíidah.

TIP

SáaHib ad-dukkáan *shopkeeper*

TIP

The expression **tfáDHDHal** and its feminine form **tfáDHDHali** are used when handing an item to someone, showing them a door or seat, and also when politely asking them to go ahead first or take their turn.

2 Decide which is true or false.

  a The first item Ali looks at is old.
  b He asks if the shopkeeper has a bigger one.
  c He then looks at a carpet.
  d He asks if it is old.

3 Match each phrase to its correct meaning.

a a-ríid a-shtári   1 of course
b háadhi jadíidah   2 this incense burner
c Táb:an   3 very beautiful
d :índ-ak tháani ákbar?   4 this (one) is new (f)
e wáajid jamíilah   5 Do you have a bigger one?
f háadha al-míjmar   6 I want to buy

4 05.03 **Listen again and repeat out loud, taking the part of Ali. You begin.**

Ali	_____
SáaHib ad-dukkáan	w :aláikum as-saláam. aish ti-ríid?
Ali	_____
Ali looks around the shop for a while.	
Ali	_____
SáaHib ad-dukkáan	(*hands one to him*) tfáDHDHal.
Ali	_____
SáaHib ad-dukkáan	laa laa, húwwa jadíid.
	(*hands him another*) háadha wáajid gadíim.
Ali	_____
SáaHib ad-dukkáan	Táb:an.
Ali looks around the shop a little more.	
Ali	_____
SáaHib ad-dukkáan	háadhi? áywa, híyya jadíidah.

Language discovery

Find the expressions in the conversation that mean:

  a bigger
  b I want to look

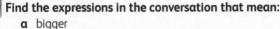

COMPARATIVE ADJECTIVES

You learned the adjective **kabíir** (*big*) in Unit 3. To say *bigger*, use the comparative form **ákbar**. Here are some adjectives with their comparative forms.

 05.04

kabíir	*big*	**ákbar**	*bigger*
Saghíir	*small*	**áSghar**	*smaller*
Tawíil	*tall, long*	**áTwal**	*taller, longer*
gaSíir	*short*	**ágSar**	*shorter*
gháali	*expensive*	**ághla**	*more expensive*
rakhíiS	*cheap*	**árkhaS**	*cheaper*
jamíil	*beautiful*	**ájmal**	*more beautiful*
zain	*good*	**áHsan**	*better*

> **TIP**
> The comparative form for adjectives is the same for both genders.

> **TIP**
> To ask for something different, use **tháani** (m) or **tháaniyah** (f).
> **:ind-ak tháani ákbar?**   *Do you* (m) *have a bigger one* (m)?
>   (lit. *with-you (a) second/ bigger (one)?*)

NUMBERS 11–20

١١	11	**iHdá:shar**
١٢	12	**ithná:shar**
١٣	13	**thalaathtá:shar**
١٤	14	**arba:atá:shar**
١٥	15	**khamsatá:shar**
١٦	16	**sittá:shar**
١٧	17	**sab:atá:shar**
١٨	18	**thamantá:shar**
١٩	19	**tis:atá:shar**
٢٠	20	**:ishríin**

1 Match the items to the Arabic.

 a

1 míjmar

 b

2 gamíiS

 c

3 zoolíyyah

 d

4 silsílah

 e

5 kháaTim

 f

6 finjáan

2 Ali needs a few more items. Separate the words, then write out his shopping list in English.

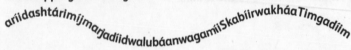

aríidashtárimijmarjadíidwalubáanwagamíiSkabíirwakháaTimgadíim

> **TIP**
>
> In Arabic, words in lists are linked by **wa** (*and*) rather than by a comma.

3 Ask the male shopkeeper the following in Arabic.

   a Do you have a smaller one (m)?

   b Do you have a cheaper one (f)?

   c Do you have a taller one (m)?

   d Do you have a shorter one (f)?

4 What do these people want to buy?

   a a-ríid a-shtári buTáagah.   **d** a-ríid sáa:ah rakhíisah.

   b :índ-ak dállah?   **e** :índ-ak gamíiS ákbar?

   c a-ríid a-shtári bánjari jamíil   **f** :índ-ak silsílah áTwal?

> **TIP**
>
> | | |
> |---|---|
> | **dállah (f)** | coffee pot |
> | **bánjari (m)** | bracelet |
> | **sáa:ah (f)** | watch, clock (also means hour) |

TALKING ABOUT PRICES

05.05 Listen and repeat, then add the missing English words.

háadha bikám?	*How much is this?* (m)
háadhi bikám?	*How much is this?* (f)
bi-khámsah riyáal	*(it costs) _____ riyals*
gháali/gháaliyah	*expensive*
fiih :índ-ak tháani árkhaS?	*Do you have a _____ one?*
ba:d gháali	*still (too) expensive*
rakhkháS-li shwáyya	*make it a little cheaper (for me)*
maa ágdar	*I can't*
laish?	*Why?*
kill shay gháali	*everything is expensive*
ti-sáwwi takhfíiDH?	*Will you give me a discount?* (lit. *you-make reduction?*)
bi-kám áakhir?	*What's (your) last (price)?*
tamáam	*OK, good*
bíshtari	*I will buy (it)*
shay tháani?	*Anything else?*

Hiwáar 2 *Conversation 2*

*05.06 Ali opts to buy an incense burner and wants to close the deal.
Listen as you read, then answer the question.*

1 How much is the first incense burner?

Ali	háadha l-míjmar al-áHmar bikám?
SáaHib ad-dukkáan	háadha ... bi-khámsah riyáal.
Ali	khámsah riyáal? gháali! fiih :índ-ak tháani árkhaS?
SáaHib ad-dukkáan	háadha bi-thaláathah riyáal.
Ali	laa, laa, laa, ba:d gháali! rakhkháS-li shwáyya!
SáaHib ad-dukkáan	ma ágdar!
Ali	laish?
SáaHib ad-dukkáan	kill shay gháali! (*said smiling*)
Ali	ti-sáwwi takhfíiDH?
SáaHib ad-dukkáan	riyaaláin wa nuSS.
Ali	(*laughs*) bikám áakhir?
SáaHib ad-dukkáan	tamáam, riyaaláin!
Ali	bíshtari. tfáDHDHal (*gives money*).
SáaHib ad-dukkáan	shúkran. shay tháani?
Ali	laa, laa, laa, shúkran.

 05.06 **Listen again and this time speak Ali's part.**

2 Find the phrases in the conversation which mean:
  a OK, two riyals.
  b Do you have a cheaper one?
  c (Will you) give me a discount?
  d This one costs three riyals.
  e Everything is expensive!
  f Anything else?

3 Read the conversation again and answer the questions.
  a What does Ali say about the price of the first item?
  b What does he say about the price of the second item?
  c Why doesn't the shopkeeper want to reduce the price?
  d What is the shopkeeper's final price?

Language discovery

1 Which part of the following phrase means *the-red-one*?

háadha l-míjmar al-áHmar bikám?

2 Which word means *two riyals*?

NOUN/ADJECTIVE PHRASES

There are rules in Arabic about using nouns and adjectives together. First, you will need to distinguish between indefinite and definite words and phrases:

▶ Indefinite words in English are preceded by *a* or *an*, but there is no word for *a* or *an* in Arabic:

bait *(a) house* **silsílah** *(a) necklace*

▶ Definite words in English are preceded by *the*:

al-bait *the house* **as-silsílah** *the necklace*

When you use an adjective with a noun to make a phrase:

a the adjective must always follow the noun.

b the adjective must agree in gender (masculine or feminine) and definiteness, *e.g. the-incense-burner, the-red-one*.

Ordinal numbers are the sole exception to this rule.

In Arabic the use or omission of **al-** (*the*) has a powerful effect on the meaning. There are three basic phrase types:

1 no al- on either word produces an indefinite phrase:

bait jadíid *(a) new house* **silsílah gadíimah** *(an) old necklace*

2 al- on both words produces a definite phrase:

al-bait al-jadíid *the new house*

as-silsílah al-gadíimah *the old necklace*

3 al- on the noun but not on the adjective produces a sentence which, in English, would contain *is* or *are*, which, as you already know, are not used in Arabic:

al-bait jadíid *the house (is) new*

as-silsílah gadíimah *the necklace (is) old*

AL-ALWÁAN *THE COLOURS*

05.07 As you learned in Units 2 and 3, adjectives in Arabic must agree
with the gender of the noun they describe. The names of the main
colours have slightly different masculine and feminine forms (first form
given is m, the second f).

ázrag/zárga (ázraq/zárqa)	*blue*	**áHmar/Hámra**	*red*
áswad/sóoda	*black*	**ábyaDH/báiDHa**	*white*
áSfar/Sáfra	*yellow*	**ákhDHar/kháDHra**	*green*

Colours ending in **-i** add **-yah** in the feminine form.

burtugáali (burtuqáali)/burtugáaliyah	*orange*
ramáadi/ramáadiyah	*grey*
wárdi/wárdiyah	*pink*
gamíiS ázrag	*a blue shirt* (**gamíiS** is masculine)
buTáagah zárga	*a blue (post)card* (**buTáagah** is feminine)

THE DUAL FORM

When you talk about two of anything in Arabic you use a special dual
form which adds **-áin** to the end of the word (or **-táin** if the word ends in
-ah). You then don't need to use the word **ithnáin** (m) or **thintáin** (f).

riyáal	*a/one riyal*	**riyaaláin**	*two riyals*
wálad	*a/one boy*	**waladáin**	*two boys*
silsílah	*a/one necklace*	**silsilatáin**	*two necklaces*

> **PRONUNCIATION TIP**
> Note that the stress moves to the end of the word in the dual form.

CURRENCIES OF THE ARABIAN GULF

Bahrain and Kuwait use the **dináar**, which is divided into 1000 **fils**.

The Omani **riyáal** (RO) is divided into 1000 **báiza**.

The Qatari **riyáal** (QR) is divided into 100 **dírham**.

The Saudi **riyáal** (SR) is divided into 100 **hálala**.

The United Arab Emirates use the **dírham** (AED or Dh), which is divided
into 100 **fils**.

05.08 Listen to the numbers and repeat them out loud.

٣٠	30	**thalaathíin**
٣٥	35	**khámsah wa thalaathíin**
٤٠	40	**arba:íin**
٥٠	50	**khamsíin**
٦٠	60	**sittíin**
٧٠	70	**sab:íin**
٨٠	80	**thamaaníin**
٩٠	90	**tis:íin**
٩٩	99	**tís:ah wa tis:íin**
١٠٠	100	**míyyah**
١٢٠	120	**míyyah w :ashríin**
٢٠٠	200	**miitáin**
٣٠٠	300	**thaláath míyyah**
٤٠٠	400	**árba: míyyah**
١٠٠	1000	**alf** (plural **aaláaf**)
٢٠٠	2000	**alfáin**
٣٠٠	3000	**thaláthah aaláaf**
١٠٠	1,000,000	**milyóon (malaayíin)**

Remember that Arabic numbers read from left to right, though groups of numbers are still shown right to left, as in these apartment numbers.

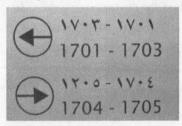

Here are two well-known Arabic story titles that include numbers. Can you guess what the stories are from their numbers?

a alf láilah wa láilah

b :áli báaba w al-arba:íin Haráami

PRACTICE 2

1 Are these colours feminine or masculine? Choose the correct form for the items below.

a zoolíyyah   áHmar/Hámra

b bánjari   burtugáali/-íyyah

c gamíiS   ákhDHar/kháDHra

d bantalóon   áswad/sóoda

e silsílah   ázrag/zárga

2 You are going on a camping holiday in Fujairah and have seen some camping equipment advertised in a local newspaper. Match the price tags to the English.

1 Dh89   2 Dh79

3 Dh50   4 Dh25

5 Dh65   6 Dh99

7 Dh42

a
٩٩ درهم

b ٨٩ درهم

c ٦٥ درهم

d ٥٠ درهم

٤٢ درهم
e

٧٩ درهم
f

٢٥ درهم
g

3 Match the Arabic numbers to their equivalent in English.

a ٩٠   1 350

b ٤٥   2 725

c ١٠٠   3 90

d ٣٥٠   4 45

e ٧٢٥   5 100

Go further

READING ARABIC

In this unit you will learn the letters **r** ر and **z** ز (**raa'** and **zaay**) and **s** س and **sh** ش (**siin** and **shiin**). They are all Sun letters.

zaay only differs from **raa'** by having one dot above it.

Both these letters are non-joiners, i.e. neither of them joins on to the following letter, and they start on the line and end below it.

siin and **shiin** are identical except that **shiin** has three dots above it. They both join on to a following letter, and are small letters on the line.

end of a word	middle of a word	start of a word	alone
أخضر **ákhDar** green	بريطانيا **briTáaniya** Britain	رخيص **rakhíiS** cheap	ر **raa'**
موز **móoz** banana	تزلج **tazálluj** skiing	زولية **zoolíyyah** carpet	ز **zaay**
شمس **shams** sun	فستان **fustáan** dress	سبعين **sab:íin** seventy	س **siin**
مشمش **míshmish** apricot	عشرة **:ásharah** ten	شمس **shams** sun	ش **shiin**

Match the transliteration to the Arabic, then find the letters raa' ر and zaay ز, siin س and shin ش in the words below. Do they appear at the beginning (B), middle (M) or end of each word (E)?

	Arabic word		Transliteration and meaning
a	درهم	1	ázraq
b	زولية	2	dináar
c	دينار	3	silsílah
d	مجمر	4	:ásharah
e	سلسلة	5	dírham
f	أزرق	6	ramáadi
g	عشرة	7	zoolíiyah
h	رمادي	8	míjimar

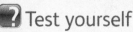

Test yourself

05.09 You are on holiday in Dubai and go to the gold suug to do some shopping. Play your part in the conversation following the prompts. Remember necklace is a feminine word!

ínta	*Greet the shopkeeper.*
SáaHib ad-dukkáan	w :aláikum as-saláam.
ínta	*Say you want to buy a necklace.*
SáaHib ad-dukkáan	*(he hands you one)* tfáDHDHal.
ínta	*Ask if he has a longer one.)*
SáaHib ad-dukkáan	áywa – tfáDHDHal.
ínta	*Say thank you, then ask if it is new.*
SáaHib ad-dukkáan	Táb:an!
ínta	*Ask how much it is.*
SáaHib ad-dukkáan	thaláath míyyah wa khamsíin dírham.
ínta	*Say it's expensive.*
Shopkeeper	kill shay gháali!
You	*Say you will buy it.*

SELF CHECK

	I CAN...
○	... ask for an item in a shop.
○	... ask for something different.
○	... say what colour something is.
○	... ask about prices.

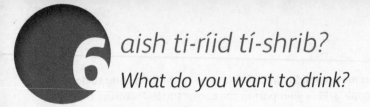

aish ti-ríid tí-shrib?

What do you want to drink?

In this unit, you will learn how to:
▶ *say what you like to eat and drink.*
▶ *say what you like and dislike, what you prefer.*
▶ *order snacks and drinks.*

CEFR: (A2) *Can interact with reasonable ease provided the other person talks slowly and clearly and is prepared to help. Can say what he or she likes and dislikes.*

Food and drink

You don't have to travel far in the Gulf to find a **dukkáan** (*small shop*) selling **mashruubáat** (*drinks*) and hot or cold **sandwiicháat**, whether in a **mool** (*mall*) in town or at a garage miles from anywhere. In the city, there is almost unlimited choice, and you will find a snack bar or **máT:am** (*restaurant*) on every corner, offering food from all around the world.

Arab hospitality is renowned, and wherever you go you will be offered **gáHwah**, **shaay** or a cold drink, and in a home, maybe some traditional **tamr** (*dates*) or fruit and often **kaik** (*cake*). Arabic coffee is much weaker than Turkish coffee, and is usually flavoured with cardamom. It is served in tiny cups, and your **finjáan** (*coffee cup*) will be refilled until you hand it back, shaking it slightly from side to side. If you are offered fruit or cake, it is considered polite to accept at least one piece, even if you have just had a big meal.

Find the Arabic word for:
a   drinks
b   sandwiches

> **TIP**
> When offered dates, take one, three or five, rather than two or four or six - it's just customary to take an odd number!

Vocabulary builder

ASKING FOR DRINKS

 06.01 Look at these words and phrases and add the missing English words to complete them. Now listen – do they sound like any English words you know?

mashruubáat	*drinks*
gáHwah	*coffee*
shaay	*tea*
... bi-Halíib/bi-l-Halíib	*... with milk*
... bi-dúun Halíib	*... without _____*
súkkar (or síkkar)	_____
:aSíir burtugáal	*orange juice*
:aSíir mángu	*mango _____*
:aSíir laimóon	*lemon juice*
... bi-na:náa:	*... _____ mint*
maay	*water*
kóola	_____

 NEW EXPRESSIONS

06.02 Look at these expressions, and note their meanings.

aish ti-ríid tí-shrib?	*What do you want to drink?*
ti-Híbb tí-shrib aish?	*What would you like to drink?*
aish :índ-kum min mashruubáat?	*What sort of drinks do you have?*
	(lit. what with-you (pl.) of drinks)
a-Híbb ...	*I like ...*
maa a-Híbb ...	*I don't like ...*
a-fáDHDHal ...	*I prefer ...*
ána áa-khudh	*I take*
ána báa-khudh	*I'll take*
Táyyib	*OK, fine, good*

Hiwaar 1 *Conversation 1*

06.03 *Mohammed is showing Lauren and Anya around Abu Dhabi when they stop at a drinks stall on the Corniche. Listen as you read, then answer the question.*

1 What doesn't Anya like?

Mohammed	aish ti-riid-íin ti-shrib-íin ya lóoran?
Lauren	aish :índ-kum min mashruubáat?
SáaHib ad-dukkáan	:índ-na gáhwah, shaay, maay, :aSíir, kóola ... kill shaay!
Lauren	ána báa-khudh shaay bi-l-Halíib min fáDHl-ak.
Mohammed	w ínti ya áanya, aish ti-riid-íin?
Anya	ána maa a-Híbb shaay. aish :índ-kum min :áSiir?
SáaHib ad-dukkáan	:índ-na :aSíir burtugáal wa mángu, wa laimóon.
Anya	ána a-fáDHDHal :aSíir laimóon bi na:náa:.
SáaHib ad-dukkáan	bi-súkkar?
Anya	ná:am, bi-súkkar min fáDHlak.
SáaHib ad-dukkáan	Táyyib. w ínta, aish ti-ríid tí-shrib?
Mohammed	ána a-Híbb :aSíir…láakin báa-khudh gáhwah.
SáaHib ad-dukkáan	Táyyib.

PRONUNCIATION TIP

In some parts of the Gulf, such as Oman, the final **-n** of **ti-riid-íin** is left out, and people say **ti-ríid-i** and **tí-shrib-i** instead.

 06.03 **Now listen again and this time speak Anya's part.**

2 Match the questions and answers.

   a aish ti-ríid tí-shrib?

   1 :índ-na :aSíir burtugáal wa mángu

   b aish :índ-kum min mashruubáat?

   2 ná:am

   c aish :índ-kum min :aSíir?

   3 ána áa-khudh gáhwah

   d ti-ríid laimóon bi-súkkar?

   4 :índ-na gáhwah, shaay…

3 True or false? Answer the following questions.

   a Lauren has tea with milk.

   b Anya likes tea.

   c The shopkeeper has three varieties of fruit juice.

   d Anya asks for lemon juice with mint.

   e Mohammed doesn't like juice.

Language discovery

1 Which Arabic words mean the same as the following?
   a What drinks have you got?
   b We have coffee.

2 Find the expressions that mean:
   a I like juice   b I don't like tea
   c I prefer coffee

1 HOW TO SAY *I HAVE*

There is no verb *to have* in Arabic. Instead, Arabs use the preposition **:ind**, meaning *with* or *in the possession of*, with the possessive pronoun suffix.

(ána) :ind-i	*I have*	(níHna) :ind-na	*we have*
(ínta) :ind-ak	*you have* (m)	(íntu) :ind-kum	*you have* (pl)
(ínti) :ind-ich	*you have* (f)		
(húwwa) :ind-uh	*he (it) has*	(húmma) :ind -hum	*they have*
(híyya) :ind-ha	*she (it) has*		

> **PRONUNCIATION TIP**
> In spoken Arabic, there's no difference between masculine and feminine in the plural.

It is common, but not essential, to say the subject or person before **:ind**:

(ána) :ind-i sayyáarah. *I have a car.* (lit. *(I) with-me (is) (a) car.*)

áHmad :ind-uh marsáidis? *Does Ahmed have a Mercedes?*
(lit. *Ahmed with-him (is) (a) Mercedes?*)

laa, :índ-uh toyóota. *No, he has a Toyota.* (lit. *no, with-him (is) (a) Toyota.*)

To say that you don't have an item, use **maa** (*not*) before the preposition.

áHmad maa :índ-uh marsáidis. *Ahmed doesn't have a Mercedes.*

2 LIKES, DISLIKES AND PREFERENCES

To say what you like, use the stem of the verb *to like* **-Hibb**, with the present tense prefixes and/or endings.

ána a-Híbb ash-shaay. *I like (the) tea.*

If you don't like something, again you use **maa** (*not*) before the verb:

(ána) maa a-Híbb al-Halíib. *(I) don't like (the) milk.*

To say you prefer something, use the verb stem **-fáDHDHal**:

ti-fáDHDHal gáhwah? áywa, a-fáDHDHal gáHwah.

Do you prefer coffee? Yes, I prefer coffee.

> **PRONUNCIATION TIP**
> With **a-fáDHDHal**, take care to pronounce both **DH**s – just leave a slight hesitation between each **DH** to be sure, as you would in *with this*.

PRACTICE 1

1 Match the Arabic to the English word for each drink.

a	shaay	**1**	mango juice
b	gáHwah	**2**	water
c	:aSíir burtugáal	**3**	coffee
d	maay	**4**	tea without sugar
e	:aSíir mángu	**5**	cola
f	:aSíir laimóon	**6**	tea
g	shaay bi-Halíib	**7**	tea with sugar
h	shaay bidúun súkkar	**8**	lemon juice
i	shaay bi-súkkar	**9**	tea with milk
j	kóola	**10**	orange juice

2 Match the Arabic to its English meaning.

a	aish :índ-ak fi sh-shánTah?	**1**	They have a boy and a girl.
b	:índ-na waladáin	**2**	Has she got a new bag?
c	:índ-ha shánTah jadíidah?	**3**	I have a big car.
d	ána :índ-i sayyáarah kabíirah	**4**	What sort of food have you got?
e	húmma :índ-hum wálad wa bint	**5**	We have two boys/sons.
f	aish :índ-kum min ákil?	**6**	What have you got in the bag?

3 Complete each sentence by adding the correct Arabic word.

a	muHámmad wa faríida _____ wálad wa bint.	**1**	:índ-na
b	náasir _____ sayyáarah saríi:ah.	**2**	:índ-hum
c	níHna maa _____ mashruubáat.	**3**	:índ-kum;
d	íntu _____ gáhwah aw shaay?	**4**	:índ-uh

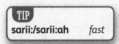

> **TIP**
> **saríi:/saríi:ah**   *fast*

Listen and understand

1 06.04 **Listen to these people ask for drinks. Which drink does each speaker want to order?**

a orange juice   **c** coffee   **e** water

b tea with sugar   **d** milk   **f** cola light

1 ___ **2** ___ **3** ___ **4** ___ **5** ___ **6** ___

> **TIP**
> **báarid**   *cold (things)*   **láait**   *light, diet*

2 06.05 **Listen to find out what the speakers prefer. Choose i or ii.**

a **i** shaay   **ii** gáHwah
b **i** :aSíir burtugáal   **ii** :aSíir laimóon
c **i** shaay bi-súkkar   **ii** shaay bidúun súkkar
d **i** Halíib   **ii** maay

3 **Now say whether or not you like each item pictured in Question 1.**

FOOD

06.06 **Listen and repeat. Then complete by adding the missing English words.**

wajibáat khafíifah	*snacks*
sandwíich (-áat)	*sandwich*
báiDHah (baiDH)	*egg (eggs)*
dajáaj	*chicken*
jíb(i)n	*cheese*
bárgar/bárghar	*burger*
má:a	*with*
baTáaTa/chibs	*chips/fries*
SálaTah	*salad*
khubz	*bread*
faláafil	_____ *(fried bean snack)*
bi-TaHíinah	*with tahini (sesame paste) dip*
bi-HúmmuS	*with _____ dip*
kaik	_____

> **TIP**
> Say **ya jamáa:ah!** as a friendly way to address a group of friends or people you know well. It means *hey, everyone!*

NEW EXPRESSIONS

ána jaw:áan/jaw:áanah.	*I am hungry.*
ínta jaw:áan?	*Are you hungry?* (to a man)
ínti jaw:áanah?	*Are you hungry?* (to a woman)
íntu jaw:aaníin?	*Are you hungry?* (plural)
aish :índ-hum min ákil?	*What have they got to eat?*
a:Tíini	*Give (to) me …*

> **TIP**
> During the Islamic month of Ramadan, most Muslims do not eat or drink anything between the hours of sunrise and sunset. It is considerate not to consume food or drink conspicuously in front of them during the day.

al-Hiin dáwr-ak! *Now your turn!*

How would a man say *I'm hungry! I'll take a burger with fries, please.*

 # Hiwáar 2 *Conversation 2*

GETTING SOMETHING TO EAT

06.07 Mohammed and some friends are going to phone a local snack bar for takeaway food, so they look at a menu. First listen, then answer the question.

1 What food do they decide to order?

Mohammed	íntu jaw:aaníin?
Fatima wa Nasser	háiwa, shwáyya.
Mohammed	aish ti-riid-úun? aish :índ-hum min ákil, yaa náasir?
Nasser	fiih sandwiicháat, SalaTáat, bárgar … :índ-hum kill shay!
Mohammed	aish ti-Hibb-íin, yaa fáaTimah?
Fatima	ána a-Híbb SálaTah bi-d-dajáaj má:a chibs.
Mohammed	zain. ti-ríid táa-kul aish ya náasir?
Nasser	maa a-ríid SálaTah. a:Tíini sandwíich bi-l-jíbin. wa muHámmad, aish ti-ríid táa-kul?
Mohammed	ána báakhudh bárgar. ya jamáa:ah! ti-riid-úun khubz wa Húmmus?
All	Táb:an!

> **TIP**
> **háiwa** (or **hái**) is a variant of **aywa**.

2 06.07 Listen again, this time speaking the part of Mohammed.

3 Match each expression in Arabic to its English meaning.

   a aish :índ-hum min ákil?   **1** Of course.
   b ti-ríid táa-kul aish?   **2** Give me a sandwich.
   c a:Tíini sandwíich   **3** What food have they got?
   d Táb:an   **4** I don't want salad.
   e maa a-ríid SálaTah   **5** What do you want to eat? (to a man)

Language discovery

Find the following in the conversation.
   1 Are you (pl) hungry?
   2 What do you want? (to more than one person)
   3 What do you want? (to a man)
   4 Do you (pl) want bread?

Now cover up your answers, and see if you can say them again without looking at the conversation.

1 PLURALS OF ADJECTIVES

To describe more than one person in Arabic, add the ending **-íin** to the adjective. There is no distinction for masculine or feminine.

:íntu jaw:aaníin?	*Are you (pl) hungry?*
áywa, níHna wáajid jaw:aaníin	*yes, we are very hungry*
w :aTshaaníin!	*and thirsty!*

> **TIP**
> :aTsháan/:aTsháanah   *thirsty (m/f)*

2 SAYING WHAT YOU WANT

a-ríid	*I want*	**na-ríid**	*we want*
ti-ríid	*you want (m)*	**ti-riid-úun**	*you (pl) want*
ti-riid-íin	*you want (f)*	**yi-riid-úun**	*they want*
yi-ríid	*he wants*		
ti-ríid	*she wants*		

PRACTICE 2

1 Match the Arabic to the English.

a sandwîich bi-d-dajáaj   **1** burger

b sandwîich bi-l-jíbin   **2** chips/fries

c sandwîich bi-l-baiDH   **3** cheese sandwich

d bárgar   **4** salad

e baTáaTa   **5** chicken sandwich

f SálaTah   **6** egg sandwich

2 What does each person prefer to eat?

a ána afáDHDHal sandwîich bi-l-jibn

b ána afáDHDHal bárgar má:a baTáaTa

c ána a-fáDHDHal faláafil bi-Hummus

3 Match each question to its correct answer.

a aish ti-ríid tí-shrab?   **1** a-ríid sandwîich bi-l-jíbin.

b ti-riid-úun gáHwah aw shaay?   **2** a-ríid áshrib kóola

c aish ti-riid-íin min sandwiicháat?   **3** na-ríid gáHwah min fáDHlich

4 Your friend Ali has dropped by. How would you ask him these questions? Match the Arabic to its English meaning.

a Are you thirsty?   **1** ti-ríid sandwîich?

b What would you like to drink?   **2** ti-fáDHDHal shaay aw gáhwah?

c Do you prefer tea or coffee?   **3** bi-l-jibin aw bi-d-dajáaj?

d With milk or sugar?   **4** ínta :aTsháan?

e Would you like a sandwich?   **5** ti-ríid tí-shrib aish?

f Cheese or chicken?   **6** bi-Halîib aw bi-súkkar?

5 Ali has brought some friends with him. How would you ask them all the same questions? Remember to use the plural form throughout.

Go further

READING ARABIC

Two pairs of letters – **S** ص and **D** ض (**Saad** and **Daad**), and **T** ط and **DH** ظ (**Taa'** and **DHaa'**) – are all Sun letters. They are all joiners, and all begin looking like an egg on its side.

The second letter of each pair has one dot above.

▶ **Saad** and **Daad** have a flourish in the separate and final forms.

▶ **Taa'** and **DHaa'** have no flourish — instead, they have an upright stick added to the left side of the egg.

end of a word	middle of a word	start of a word	alone
رخيص **rakhíiS** *cheap*	عصير **:aSíir** *juice*	صغير **Saghíir** *small*	ص **Saad**
بيض **baiD** *eggs*	أخضر **ákhDar** *green*	ضيف **Daif** *guest*	ض **Daad**
وسط **wásaT** *middle*	مطعم **máT:am** *restaurant*	طعام **Ta:áam** *food*	ط **Taa'**
حظ **HaDHDH** *luck*	نظيف **naDHíif** *clean*	أبو ظبي **ábu DHábi** *Abu Dhabi*	ظ **DHaa'**

> **TIP**
> Remember, the letter **Daad** is usually pronounced like the letter **DHaa'** in the Gulf, so **baiDH** (*eggs*) is actually spelled **baiD** in written form.

1 **Look at the Arabic words and find the letters Saad and Daad, Taa' and DHaa'. Do they appear at the beginning (B), middle (M) or end (E) of these words?**

	Arabic		English
a	قطر	1	ábu **DH**ábi (Abu Dhabi)
b	طيب	2	á**S**far (yellow)
c	قميص	3	bái**D**ah (an egg)
d	الظهران	4	qamíi**S** (a shirt)
e	أبو ظبي	5	Hoo**D** (tank)
f	بيضة	6	a**DH-DH**ahrán (Dhahran)
g	أصفر	7	qá**T**ar (Qatar)
h	حوض	8	**T**áyyib (fine, ok)

2 **Now match the Arabic words to their transliteration.**

3 Read each sign and match it to its meaning. Remember to look
   for letters you have learned in this unit.

a مطعم

b خروج فقط

c ممنوع التصوير

1 exit only (kharúuj fáqaT)

2 no photography
   (mamnúu: at-taSwíir)

3 restaurant (máT:am)

Test yourself

 You go into a café for a snack and a drink. Following the prompts, give the most appropriate reply.

SáaHib ad-dukkáan	masáa' al-khair.
ínta	*Reply appropriately and ask what they've got to drink.*
SáaHib ad-dukkáan	:índ-na shaay, gáhwah, :aSíir, kóola …
ínta	*Ask what kinds of juice they have.*
SáaHib ad-dukkáan	:índ-na :aSíir burtugáal wa tufáH, wa laimóon.
ínta	*Say you'll take an apple juice. Ask what kind of sandwiches they have.*
SáaHib ad-dukkáan	fiih sandwiicháat bi-l-jíbin, bi-d-dajáaj, bi-l-báiDH, wa fiih bárgar
ínta	*Ask him to give you a burger and fries.*
SáaHib ad-dukkáan	má:a SálaTah?
ínta	*Tell him no, without salad.*
SáaHib ad-dukkáan	(a few minutes later) tfáDHDHal.
ínta	*Make an appropriate reply.*

SELF CHECK

	I CAN...
○	... say what I like to eat and drink.
○	... say what I like and dislike, what I prefer.
●	... order snacks and drinks.

R2 Review: Units 4–6

 1 **Complete each Arabic sentence, saying out loud the time shown.**
   a 3:00 = as-sáa:ah_____.
   b 5:10 = as-sáa:ah khámsah_____ :áshar.
   c 7:30 = as-sáa:ah_____ wa_____.
   d 9:45 = as-sáa:ah :ásharah_____ rúba:.

2 **Do these times occur in the morning (am) or evening (pm)?**
   a as-sáa:ah khámsah aS-SúbaH.
   b as-sáa:ah thaláathah fi l-lail.
   c as-sáa:ah thintáin ba:d aDH-DHuhr.
   d as-sáa:ah sáb:ah aS-SúbaH.

3 **You have just arrived at your hotel in Doha. It's hot and you fancy a swim. Ask the receptionist if there is a pool in the hotel.**

4 **Rank the days of the week in order from Sunday (1) to Saturday (7).**
   a yoom al-júma:ah
   b yoom ath-thaláathah
   c yoom al-árba:ah
   d yoom as-sabt
   e yoom al-áHad
   f yoom al-khamíis
   g yoom al-ithnáin

5 **Unjumble each sentence so it makes sense in Arabic.**
   a kam as-síinima as-sáa:ah tíftaH?
   b as-sáa:ah yibánnid al-máT:am kam?
   c wa al-mool as-sáa:ah nuss yíftaH tís:ah.
   d al-másbaH yibánnid as-sáa:ah sáb:ah fi l-lail.

Now say each sentence out loud.

6 Match each number in Arabic to its correct numeral in the box. Careful! Two more numerals than necessary have been provided.

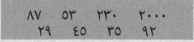

| ٨٧ | ٥٣ | ٢٣٠ | ٢٠٠٠ |
| ٢٩ | ٤٥ | ٣٥ | ٩٢ |

a	thaláathah wa khamsíin	_____
b	khámsah wa arba:íin	_____
c	miitáin wa thalathíin	_____
d	tís:ah wa :ashríin	_____
e	sáb:ah wa thamaníin	_____
f	alfáin	_____

 Now say these numbers out loud in Arabic and English.

7 All Arabic nouns are either masculine or feminine. Complete these statements on grammar by selecting the correct Arabic word.

a For masculine nouns you use **húwwa/híyya** to say _it (is)_, and **háadha/háadhi** to say _this (is)_.

b For feminine nouns you use **húwwa/híyya** to say _it (is)_, and **háadha/háadhi** to say _this (is)_.

8 Decide whether each of these nouns is masculine (M) or feminine (F), then give the correct English meaning of each.

a	kháaTim	**c**	míjmar	**e**	fustáan
b	silsílah	**d**	buTáagah	**f**	gamíiS

9 Lara did the homework for her Arabic course in a rush and forgot to change háadha to háadhi for the feminine words. She also got some of her adjective endings muddled up. Help Lara by suggesting corrections, where appropriate. Did she get any right?

a _háadha zoolíyyah jamíil._ ❏ _____

b _háadha míjmar kabíir._ ❏ _____

c _háadha finjáan rakhíiSah._ ❏ _____

d _haadha silsílah Tawíil._ ❏ _____

Now translate each sentence into English.

10 **What is the meaning of these adjectives in English? Match each adjective to its comparative form in Arabic.**

a	kabíir	_____	1	ágSar
b	Saghíir	_____	2	áTwal
c	rakhíiS	_____	3	áSghar
d	gháali	_____	4	ákbar
e	gaSíir	_____	5	árkhaS
f	Tawíil	_____	6	ághla
g	jamíil	_____	7	ájmal

 11 **Ask out loud in Arabic for a different item using the comparative adjectives in the previous exercise. Use the masculine form for each.**

Example: :índ-ak tháani árkhaS? (*Do you have a cheaper one?*)

12 **Add the correct ending for the preposition :índ (*with*), following the prompts in English.**

a	:índ _____	I have (lit. with-me, etc.)
b	:índ _____	he has
c	:índ _____	we have
d	:índ _____	they have
e	:índ _____	you (f) have

13 **Match the English to the Arabic.**

a	:índ-ak gamíiS ábyaDH?	1	This is a blue car.
b	:háadhi sayyáarah zárgah.	2	Where is the green apple?
c	wain at-tufáaHah al-kháDHra?	3	I want to buy the black car.
d	a-ríid a-shtári as-sayyáarah as-sóoda.	4	Do you have a white shirt?

 14 **You are in a café. Ask the waiter in Arabic for these items.**

a I'd like _____ please.

b I'll take   please.

c Give me   please.

15 Which is the odd one out and why?
a al-ithnáin   as-sabt   al-áHad   al-fúndug
b khamsíin   saba:íin   thaláathah   :ashríin
c áHmar   zoolíyyah   burtugáali   áswad
d :aSíir laimóon   kaik   faláafil   khubz

16 Simon got a speeding ticket whilst driving along this road.
How fast was he going?
a 40 km/**h**   **b** 50km/h   **c** 60km/h

17 You see these signs while shopping. Match them to their pronunciation and English meaning.

a المخرج   _____

b نعناع   _____

c مفتوح   _____

d تنزيلات   _____

e شـاي   _____

f تفاح   _____

g طماطم   _____

h برتقال   _____

A tanziiláat (reductions/discounts)		**1** apple
B TamáaTim		**2** tea
C burtuqáal		**3** exit
D al-múkhrij (exit)		**4** mint
E tuffáaH		**5** orange
F shaay		**6** tomato
G na:náa:		**7** open
H maftúuH		**8** reductions/discounts

7 fi l-madíinah
In the city

In this unit you will learn how to:
▶ *ask for places in a town.*
▶ *ask where places are.*
▶ *ask for and give directions.*
▶ *direct a taxi driver to your destination.*

CEFR: (A2) *Can deal with common aspects of everyday living such as travel. Can ask for and understand simple directions relating to how to get from X to Y, by foot or public transport.*

🔘 Getting around the city

Most Gulf cities were laid out during the 1970s and 1980s, mainly as a result of the rocketing price of oil. Development is ongoing throughout the region and many cities are ultra-contemporary, with clusters of **abráaj** (*towers*) of dizzying heights and futuristic designs crowding the skyline. In contrast, others are more traditional, their history and heritage evident at every turn. Each district has its own **másjid** (*mosque*), often more than one, and it won't be long before you become accustomed to the sound of the **adháan** (*Islamic call to prayer*) five times a day. Cities such as Dubai and Sharjah grew up around creeks, and these and other coastal cities have a **míina** (*port* or *harbour*) and a **suug as-sámak**. And, wherever you are, you are sure to stumble across a **mool** or two!

Getting around is fun once you have mastered a few simple phrases such as **wain as-suug?** (*Where is the souq?*) and **fiih dukkáan garíib min hína?** (*Is there a shop near here?*). If you know your **yisáar** (*left*) from your **yamíin** (*right*), you will soon find your way around **wásaT al-madíinah** (*the centre of town*) without getting lost.

 If **sámak** means *fish*, what is a **suug as-sámak**?

V Vocabulary builder

07.01 Listen, then complete the English translation by adding the missing words.

fi l-madíinah	in the city
al-báHar	the sea/beach
al-khoor	the creek
al-jísir	the bridge
al-másjid	the _____
al-mátHaf	the museum
al-maTáar	the airport
*ash-sháari:	the street
*aS-Saydalíiyah	the pharmacy
*as-súubermarkit	the _____
suug *as-sámak	the fish _____

> **PRONUNCIATION TIP**
> *Remember that all these words begin with a Sun letter, so the **laam** in **al-** (*the*)
> is silent, and the first letter is clearly doubled.

al-ittijaháat	directions
ruuH	go! (m)
rúuHi	go! (f)
liff	turn! (m)
líffi	turn! (f)
khudh	take! (m)
khúdhi	take! (f)
síidah	straight on
yamíin	right
yiSáar (also shimáal)	left
:ála l-yisáar	on the _____
:ála l-yamíin	on the _____

V NEW EXPRESSIONS

07.02 Listen and repeat out loud, trying to match the speakers' pronunciation.

law samáHt	please, excuse me (to a man)
law samáHti	please, excuse me (to a woman)
garíib/garíibah (qaríib/qaríibah)	near (m/f)
fíih bank garíib min hína?	Is there a bank near here?

al-bank ba:íid :an hína?	*(Is) the bank far from here?*
tá:raf sháari: …?	*Do you know … street?*
maa á:raf	*I don't know*
ba:dáin	*then, after that*
muu ákthar	*not more*
maa fiih	*there isn't*

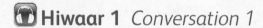

Hiwaar 1 *Conversation 1*

07.03 *Suresh is spending the afternoon in Muscat and needs to find a bank. He asks a passer-by for help. First listen, then answer the question.*

1 What is the first direction the man gives to Suresh?

Suresh	law samáHt, fiih bank garíib min hína?
rajjáal	áywa fiih. tá:raf sháari: al-bustáan?
Suresh	laa, maa á:raf.
rajjáal	zain. ruuH síidah wa ba:dáin liff yamíin. al-bank :ála l-yisáar.
Suresh	al-bank ba:íid :an hína?
rajjáal	laa laa, húwwa garíib. khams dagáayig bass, muu ákthar.
Suresh	shúkran. wa fiih baríid garíib min hína?
rajjáal	laa, maa fiih.
Suresh	shúkran.
rajjáal	:áfwan

> **TIP**
>
> You already know how to say *please* (**min fáDHl-ak/-ich**). The phrase **law samáHt** (to a man) and **law samáHti** (to a woman) is a more polite or formal way of saying please, and is often used to mean *excuse me* when you want to attract someone's attention, such as in a restaurant.

2 Match the Arabic to the English.

a	left	**1**	yamíin
b	near	**2**	síidah
c	right	**3**	garíib
d	straight on	**4**	yisáar

3 Find the Arabic phrases that mean:
   a No, I don't know.
   b Go straight.
   c Then turn right.
   d Is the bank far from here?

4 Are these statements true or false?
   a Suresh knows where al-Bustaan street is.
   b First he must go straight.
   c The bank is on the left.
   d The bank is ten minutes away.

Language discovery

1 Find the Arabic phrases that mean:
   a Is there a post office near here?
   b No, there isn't.

2 Find the Arabic phrase that means *Go straight.*

1 THERE IS AND THERE ARE

It is very easy to say *there is* and *there are* in Arabic – just use the word **fiih**. The **h** is silent, but is written this way to distinguish it from the word **fii** meaning *in*. Remember, there is no word for *a* or *an*.

fiih fúndug.	*There is a hotel.*
fiih fúndug fii dubáy.	*There is a hotel in Dubai.*

To express *there is not* or *there are not*, you say **maa fiih**.

maa fiih fúndug garíib min hína. *There isn't a hotel near here.*

REGIONAL VARIATIONS OF FIIH

Mainly in Bahrain you will hear the Persian borrowing **hast** instead of **fiih**, and in Kuwait and Iraq they say **áku**.

---

2 TELLING PEOPLE TO DO SOMETHING

These forms of the verb (known as imperatives) are frequently used in giving directions. Those you will learn in this unit are:

ruuH!	*go!*
liff!	*turn!*
khudh!	*take!*

Imperative verb forms have to be altered according to the person spoken to, so you add **-i** if you are talking to a woman and **-u** if you are talking to more than one person of either gender.

	masculine	feminine	plural
go	**ruuH**	**rúuHi**	**rúuHu**
turn	**liff**	**líffi**	**líffu**
take	**khudh**	**khúdhi**	**khúdhu**

 PRACTICE 1

1 There are five places about town mentioned in this word-snake. Can you find them? Then mark the stress on each word where appropriate.

fundugmarkazashshurTahmaT:amSaydaliyyahmustashfa

2 Match each direction to its correct symbol.

  a síidah   1 ←
  b yisáar   2 →
  c yamíin   3 ↑

3 Match the Arabic to the English.

  a laa, maa fiih.   1 Where is the airport?
  b al-maTáar min wain?   2 Is there a restaurant near here?
  c fiih máT:am garíib min hína?   3 Go straight then left.
  d ruuH síidah wa ba:dáin liff yisáar.   4 No, there isn't.

4 Which imperative verb would you use to complete each sentence?

  a ruuH/liff yisáar.
  b ruuH/liff síidah.
  c ruuH/liff yamíin.

 5 You are out and about in town. Ask a passer-by if each of these places is nearby. Remember to use garíibah for feminine words.

> **PRONUNCIATION TIP**
>
> You don't need to use **al-** as you are asking for *a* post office rather than *the* post office.
> **Example: fiih baríid garíib min hína?**   *Is there a post office near here?*

a	post office (m)	**e**	hotel (m)
b	hospital (f)	**f**	pharmacy (f)
c	police station (m)	**g**	school (f)
d	museum (m)	**h**	fish market (m)

5 Now repeat Question 5, this time asking if each place is far from here. Remember to use ba:íidah for feminine nouns.

Example: al-baríid ba:íid :an hína?   *Is the post office far from here?*

Listen and understand

1 07.04 Listen to these people talk about places in town. Where does each person want to go? Choose from the following list, then say if there is (fiih) or is not (maa fiih) such a place in town.

> market   cinema   museum   pharmacy
> shop   hospital   hotel

a _____	e _____
b _____	f _____
c _____	g _____
d _____	

2 07.05 Where are the speakers going and how do they get there? For example, to get to A the speaker must use Directions 3.

1 ↑←   **2** ↑   **3** → ←   **4** → ↑

a _____	c _____
b _____	d _____

NEW EXPRESSIONS

07.06 First listen, then add the missing words.

al-fúndug min wain?	*Where is the _____?*
kaif a-rúuH al-fúndug?	*How do I get to _____?*
áwwal yamíin	*(the) first _____*
tháani yiSáar	*(the) second _____*
:ind ad-duwwáar	*at the roundabout*
laa tísra:l	*Don't speed up!*
muu mushkílah!	*No problem!*

Hiwáar 2 *Conversation 2*

07.07 *Anya is lost in Ruwi because the taxi driver can't find her hotel. She winds down the window to ask a passer-by. First listen, then answer the question.*

1 What is the name of Anya's hotel?

Anya	law samáHt, fúndug ash-shams min wain?
rajjáal	*(scratching his chin)* khalíini afákkir ... rúuHi síida, wa :ind ad-duwwáar líffi yamíin wa ba:dáin khúdhi tháani sháari: :ála l-yamíin.
Anya	zain, wa ba:dáin?
rajjáal	fúndug ash-shams bá:d khamsíin mítir, jamb máT:am aS-SaHaráa'.
Anya	shúkran. wa kaif arúuH al-báHar min al-fúndug?
rajjáal	al-báHar wáajid garíib – min al-fúndug khúdhi áakhir sháari: :ála l-yisáar. yá:ani ... thaláath dagáayig bass.
Anya	Hayyáa-k Al-láah.
rajjáal	fii amáan Al-láah.
The taxi driver speeds up.	
Anya	*(shouting)* shwáyya shwáyya, laa tísra:l
sawwáag	muu mushkílah!

TIP	
sawwáag (at-táaksi)	*(taxi) driver*
rajjáal	*man*
khallíini afákkir	*let me think*

2 What does Anya say to the taxi driver at the end?

> **Hayyáa-k Al-láah** is a well-wishing phrase, literally meaning *God give you life*. It can mean *goodbye* or *thank you*, depending on the context. The response **fii amáan Al-láah** means *May God keep you safe*.

 07.07 **Listen again and speak Anya's part.**

3 Complete the notes for Anya's directions in English.

Go _____, then at the _____, turn _____, then take the _____ street on the _____. The Sun Hotel is after _____ metres, next to the Desert _____.

Language discovery

Find the phrases in the conversation which mean:
- **a** take the second street on the right
- **b** next to the Desert Restaurant

1 ORDINAL NUMBERS

Ordinal numbers tell us what order things are in, i.e. *first, second, third* and so on. They are commonly used when giving directions.

áwwal	*first*	**sáadis**	*sixth*
tháani	*second*	**sáabi:**	*seventh*
tháalith	*third*	**tháamin**	*eighth*
ráabi:	*fourth*	**táasi:**	*ninth*
kháamis	*fifth*	**:áashir**	*tenth*

You might also need the word **áakhir**, meaning *last*, as in **áakhir sháari: :ála l-yamíin** (*last street on the right*).

Unlike normal adjectives, which come after the noun, ordinal numbers can sometimes appear before the noun, especially when giving directions.

2 PREPOSITIONS

Prepositions are words that tell us the position of something.

Arabic	English	Example
fii	*in*	**fi l-madíinah*** *in the city*
:ála	*on*	**:ála l-yisáar*** *on the left*
:ind	*at, by*	**:ind ad-duwwáar** *at the roundabout*
jamb	*next to*	**jamb al-máT:am** *next to the restaurant*
gábil (qábil)	*before*	**gábil al-jísir** *before the bridge*
bá:d	*after*	**bá:d al-jísir** *after the bridge*
amáam	*in front of*	**amáam al-bait** *in front of the house*
wára	*behind*	**wára s-sayyáarah*** *behind the car*
foog	*up, above*	**íTla: foog** *go up*; **foog ad-dukkáan** *above the shop*
táH(i)t	*down, under*	**ínzil taH(i)t** *go down*; **táH(i)t al-jísir** *under the bridge*

> **TIP**
> *If a word beginning with **al-** (*the*) follows **fii**, **:ála** or **wára**, the two words slide into each other and the **a** in **al-** (*the*) is not pronounced.

 PRACTICE 2

1 Match the Arabic to the English.

a	fii	**1**	on
b	gábil	**2**	behind
c	:ála	**3**	in
d	foog	**4**	under
e	jamb	**5**	above
f	taHt	**6**	at
g	wára	**7**	before
h	:ind	**8**	next to

 2 How would you say the following to a man?

a Take the first street on the right.

b Take the third street on the left.

c Take the fourth street on the right then turn left.

d Take the second street on the right then go straight.

e At the roundabout turn left.

3 Repeat Exercise 2, but respond as if you were talking to a woman.

 4 07.08 **Listen to these speakers, then answer the questions.**
   a Where does he want to go?
   b What directions is he given?
   c How far is it?
   d Where is it exactly?

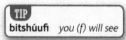

> **TIP**
> **bitshúufi** *you (f) will see*

5 How would you say the following in Arabic? Some of the words you will need are given in the box. Remember there is no word for *is*.

Example: a al-wálad fi l-máT:am.

> **al-wálad   al-baríid   aS-Saydalíyyah   al-másjid**
> **as-sayyáarah   al-fúndug   as-síinima   al-mátHaf   al-jísir**

   a The boy is in the restaurant.
   b The cinema is after the police station.
   c The post office is before the supermarket.
   d The pharmacy is next to the museum.
   e The car is under the bridge.
   f The hotel is after the mosque.

Go further

 READING ARABIC

In this unit you will learn to read and recognize the letters **:** ع (**:ain**) and **gh** غ (**ghain**). These letters are identical in shape, a big bulge below a smaller bulge, except that **ghain** has a dot above it. Learn them as a pair and, as with all the other letters you have learned, practise spotting and distinguishing between them whenever you see written Arabic. This is what they look like on their own, at the start, in the middle and at the end of a word.

end of a word	middle of a word	start of a word	on its own
سريع **saríi:** *fast*	بعد **ba:d** *after*	عنب **:ínab** *grapes*	ع **:ain**
مبلغ **máblagh** *amount*	صغير **Saghíir** *small*	غالي **gháali** *expensive*	غ **ghain**

1 Complete the English meaning and transliteration for the Arabic words in the table.

	English meaning	Transliteration	Arabic
a		*sháari:*	شارع
b	*language*		لغة
c		*:ála*	على
d		*ba:dáin*	بعدين
e	*juice*		عصير
f		*gháali*	غالي
g	*Oman*		عمان
h		*baghdáad*	بغداد

2 How would you write the Arabic title at the top of the Arabic script column?

3 Now highlight the letters :ain and ghain in each Arabic word.

4 You see these signs at a petrol station. Which sign says:

a :áadi *regular (petrol)*

b mamnúu: at-tadkhíin *no smoking*?

1    2

❓ Test yourself

1 Complete this conversation by adding the correct words from the box.

fiih	rúuH	samáHt	tháani	ba:d
yamíin	:ála	as-suug	wain	maa

ínta	law _____, al-mátHaf al-isláami min _____?
rajjáal	_____ síida, wa :ind ad-duwwáar liff _____ wa
	ba:dáin khudh _____ sháari: _____ l-yamíin.
ínta	zain, wa ba:dáin?
rajjáal	al-mátHaf _____ khamsíin mítir, jamb _____.
ínta	wa _____ bank garíib min hína?
rajjáal	laa, _____ fiih.

2 How would you ask the following in Arabic?
   a Is there is a restaurant near here?
   b Where is the sea?
   c How do I get to the cinema from here?

3 How would you say the following in Arabic?
   a Go straight on (to a man).
   b Turn left then go straight (to a woman).
   c Go straight then take the second right (to a man).
   d No, there isn't a bank near here.
   e The fish market is next to the harbour.

SELF CHECK

I CAN. . .
... ask for places in a town.
....ask where places are.
... ask for and give directions.
...direct a taxi driver to my destination.

8 li-wain?

Where to?

In this unit you will learn how to:
▶ *book and buy travel tickets.*
▶ *hire a car.*
▶ *buy petrol and deal with simple car problems.*

CEFR: (A2) *Can get simple information about travel, use public transport such as buses, trains and taxis, and buy tickets.*

📷 Getting out and about

Thanks to heavily-subsidized **banzíin** (*petrol*) prices in the Gulf states, travel by **at-táaksi** is cheap and easy and you won't have to wait long for one in most major cities. Many taxis have meters these days, but if not, before getting inside, you should ask the price – **tirúuH as-suug bikám?** (*How much to the market?*) Dubai has a clean and modern **mítru** system, and its immaculate carriages are, like the city's buses, fully air-conditioned and include separate ladies-only sections. In some Gulf countries, **baaS** (*bus*) services are very sporadic, but in others there is a well-established and modern bus network with a frequent service. Waiting at the **máwgif al-baaS** can get a little hot during summer months, but some are enclosed and air-conditioned. Long-distance buses are a cheap and convenient way to travel across the region or of course you can go by **Tayyáarah** (*plane*).

Once at your destination you could hire a **sayyáarah** or a **foor-wiil** and take off into the **SaHaráa'** or **barr** (*desert*) for the weekend. In coastal areas, another popular way to get around is to travel by **márkib** (*boat*), whether to get from A to B, such as the one-dirham **:ábrah** crossing Dubai creek, or simply for pleasure to experience an afternoon on the stunning waters of the Arabian Gulf itself.

Find the Arabic for:
a   metro
b   bus stop

Ⓥ Vocabulary builder

08.01 First read, then add the missing English words. Then listen and repeat these expressions.

as-sáfar	*travel*
baaS (-áat)	*bus*
sayyáarah (-áat)	*car*
táaksi (-yáat)	_____
giTáar (qiTáar) (-áat)	*train*
mítru	_____
Tayyáarah (-áat)	*plane*
tádhkarah (tadháakir)	*ticket (tickets)*
dhiháab	*one way* (lit. *going*)
dhiháab w iyáab	*return* (lit. *going and coming back*)
mubáasharatan	*direct*

NEW EXPRESSIONS

08.02 First read, then add the missing English words. Then listen and repeat these expressions.

fiih baaS yirúuH ad-dóoHah?	*Is there a _____ that goes to Doha?*
fiih baaS yirúuH ...	*There is (a) bus (which) goes ...*
mubáasharatan	*direct* (lit. *there (is) bus it-goes directly*)
al-baaS yíTla: as-sáa:ah thintáin	*the bus leaves at _____ o'clock*
máta?	*When?*
yóoSal (m) al-baaS	*the bus arrives* (m)
tóoSal (f) aT-Tayyáarah	*the _____ arrives* (f)
Hagg báakir (báachir)	*for tomorrow*
múmkin ádfa: bi l-kart?	*Can I pay by credit card?*
múmkin	*it's possible*

> **TIP**
> Now that you have got used to the verb prefixes and suffixes, these and the stress in each word will only be shown in the Vocabulary builder and New expressions, i.e. from this unit on you will see **yiruuH** rather than **yi-rúuH**.

 **Hiwaar 1** *Conversation 1*

08.03 *Ahmed, a Saudi student in Riyadh, is travelling to visit his parents, who live in Doha. He doesn't want to fly, so he goes to the bus station to ask about the bus service to Doha. First listen, then answer the question.*

1 Does Ahmed want a single or return ticket?

Ahmed	fiih baaS yiruuH ad-dooHah min faDH-lak?
kaatib	aywa, fiih baaS yiruuH mubaasharatan.
Ahmed	at-tadhkarah bi-kam?
kaatib	dhihaab bass aw dhihaab w iyaab?
Ahmed	dhihaab w iyaab.
kaatib	miyyah wa khamsah wa :ishriin riyaal.
Ahmed	al-baaS yiTla: as-saa:ah kam?
kaatib	yiTla: as-saa:ah thamaanyah aS-SubaH bi DH-DHabt.
Ahmed	zain, wa mata yooSal ad-dooHah?
kaatib	yooSal as-saa:ah sab:ah wa nuSS al-misa.
Ahmed	nzain. a:Tiini tadhkarat dhihaab w iyaab Hagg baakir. mumkin adfa: bi l-kart?
kaatib	aywa, mumkin.

 08.03 **Listen again, and this time speak the part of Ahmed.**

> **PRONUNCIATION TIP**
> The word **zain** (*good, fine*) is sometimes pronounced with an **n**-sound in front of it to make **nzain**.

2 True or false?
   a The ticket costs 120 Riyals.
   b The bus leaves at 8 o'clock in the evening.
   c He wants a ticket for tomorrow.

3 Find the Arabic expressions that mean:
   a There is a bus that goes direct.
   b How much is the ticket?
   c What time does the bus leave?
   d When does it arrive in Doha?
   e Give me a return ticket for tomorrow.

Language discovery

1 How do you say in Arabic *Give me a return ticket*?

2 How do you say in Arabic *Is there is a bus which goes to Doha, please?*

> **TIP**
> The expression *Give me …* used when asking for something might seem a little rude or abrupt in English, but this is not the case in Arabic.

1 POSSESSIVE PHRASES

You have already learned the possessive suffixes **-i**, **-ak**, **-ich**, etc. to express the idea of belonging, such as **aish ism-ak?** *What's your name?* (to a man).

You can also express belonging in Arabic by placing two nouns together, the second one usually having **al** (*the*) in front of it. Here are some possessive phrases you have already come across.

ragam at-tilifoon	*telephone number* (lit. *number of the telephone*)
sawwaag at-taaksi	*taxi driver* (lit. *driver of the taxi*)
mawgif al-baaS	*bus stop* (lit. *stop of the bus*)
wasaT al-madiinah	*town centre* (lit. *centre of the town*)
suug as-samak	*fish market* (lit. *market of the fish*)

Note that if a feminine noun ending in **-ah** is used as the first part of such a construction it changes to **-at**, as in **tadhkarat dhihaab w iyaab** *a return ticket*.

madiinat al-kuwait	*Kuwait City* (lit. *city of (the) Kuwait*)
sayyaarat al-mudiir	*the manager's car* (lit. *car of the manager*)
saa:at al-jaami:ah	*the university clock*

In the first word in this construction, never place **al-** in front of it. Instead, always place **al-** in front of the second word unless it is a proper noun, such as a name, as in this example:

naadi dubay li s-sayyidaat	*Dubai Ladies Club* (lit. *club of Dubai for the ladies*)

The indefinite equivalent of such possessive phrases can be seen in the following example.

sawwaag taaksi	*a taxi driver*

2 PLURALS – TALKING ABOUT MORE THAN TWO THINGS

You will have noticed that some nouns in the Vocabulary builder in this unit have something in brackets after them, e.g. **sayyaarah (-aat)** and **tadhkarah (tadhaakir)**. For most words ending in **-ah**, which are usually but not always feminine in gender, you often form the plural by removing the **-ah** and adding **-aat**. But some words, like **tádhkarah**, change their internal shape, e.g. **tadháakir**. Plurals are explained in further detail in *Complete Spoken Arabic* and *Complete Arabic*. For now, you need only learn the plural form with the noun and notice the different forms as you come across them in the glossary. And remember to use the special dual form for two of anything, as explained in Unit 5.

 PRACTICE 1

1 Match the Arabic to the correct English translation.

a tadhkarat thihaab w iyaab   **1** there's no train to Kuwait

b fiih baaS yiruuH mubaasharatan   **2** how much is a single ticket?

c yooSal as-saa:ah thintain   **3** a return ticket

d maa fiih giTaar yiruuH al-kuwait   **4** it arrives at two o'clock

e tadhkarat dhihaab bass bikam?   **5** there's a direct bus

2 Complete each sentence by adding the correct word from the box.

> iyaab   mubaasharatan   mata   Hagg
> yiruuH   bi-kam   yiTla: as-saa:ah

a fiih baaS _____ ad-dooHah min faDHlak?

b maa fiih baaS yiruuH _____.

c at-tadhkarah _____?

d dhihaab bass aw dhihaab w _____?

e al-baaS _____ as-saa:ah kam?

f wa _____ yoosal dubay?

g yooSal _____ sab:ah wa nuSS fi l-misa.

h a:Tiini tadhkarat dhihaab w iyaab _____ baakir.

106

3 Look at the Muscat to Dubai bus timetable, then say if the following statements are true or false.

Buses from Muscat to Dubai		
Muscat, Ruwi Bus Station	dep	0730
Muscat International Airport		0755
Barka Roundabout		0830
Sohar – Shell Station	arr	1005
Sohar – Shell Station	dep	1025
Wajajah – border post	arr	1125
Dubai – Dnata car park	arr	1325

a yiTla: min masqaT as-saa:ah saba:ah wa nuSS.

b yooSal fii SoHaar as-saa:ah :asharah wa thilth.

c al-baaS yiruuH mubaasharatan.

d yooSal fii dubay as-saa:ah :waaHidah wa nuSS illa khams.

4 Match the Arabic to its English translation.
a	mool al-imaaraat	1	the gold market
b	mawaagif as-sayyaaraat	2	shopping centre
c	markaz tijaari	3	Sharjah University
d	jaami:at ash-shaarjah	4	Mall of the Emirates
e	suug adh-dhahab	5	the car park

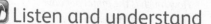 Listen and understand

1 08.04 What type of ticket does each traveller want? First listen, then select the correct ticket type.
   a one-way/return ticket
   b one-way/return ticket
   c one-way/return ticket
   d one-way/return ticket

2 Ask if there is a bus to each destination.
  a Abu Dhabi
  b Muscat
  c Riyadh
  d Salalah

 3 You want to take a train from Dammam to Riyadh. Speak your part of the conversation, following the prompts. You begin.

Say good morning.
SabaaH an-nuur.
Ask if there is a train to Riyadh tomorrow afternoon.
na:am, fiih giTaar yiruuH mubaasharatan.
Ask what time it leaves.
yiTla: as-saa:ah thintain ba:d aDH-DHuhr.
Ask what time it arrives in Riyadh.
yooSal as-saa:ah waaHidah fi l-lail.
Ask how much a return ticket costs.
miyyah wa thalaathiin riyaal.

 NEW EXPRESSIONS

 08.05 First add the missing English words, then listen and repeat the phrases.

a-ríid astá'jir sayyáarah	I'd like to hire a car.
a-ríid astá'jir foor-wiil	I'd like to hire a _____ car.
fii-ha al-sii?	Does it have A/C?
li-múddat aish?	For how long?
kam al-iijáar fi l-yoom?	How much is the rental per day?
kam al-iijáar li-...	How much is the rental for ...
... yoom wáaHid/yoomáin/usbúu:?	... a _____/two _____/a week?
si:r makhSúuS	special price
tfáDHDHal al-láisan máal-i	Here's my driving licence.
háadha s-sí:r má:a t-ta'míin?	Does this price include insurance?
as-sáa:ah kam láazim arajjí:-ha?	What time must I return it?

Hiwáar 2 *Conversation 2*

08.06 *Louis is in Sharjah and decides to rent a car for the weekend. He arrives at the rental office and speaks to the clerk. First listen, then answer the question.*

1 What kind of car does Louis want to rent?

Louis	ariid asta'jir sayyaarah foor-wiil min faDHlak.
káatib	:ind-na toyoota praado jadiidah. hiyya sayyaarah waajid jamiilah!
Louis	fii-ha ai-sii?
kaatib	Tab:an!
Louis	kam al-iijaar fi l-yoom?
káatib	dagiigah min faDHlak ... al-iijaar thalaath miyyah dirham fi l-yoom. tiriid-ha li-muddat aish?
Louis	li-yoomain.
káatib	zain. a:Tiik si:r makhSuuS. khams miyyah wa khamsiin dirham bass.
Louis	haadha s-si:r ma:a t-ta'miin?
káatib	dagiigah min faDHlak ... na:am as-si:r ma:a t-ta'miin.
Louis hands over his driver's licence.	
Louis	tfaDHDHal al-laisan maal-i. as-saa:ah kam laazim arajji:-ha?
káatib	yoom as-sabt, nafs al-wagt ... ya:ani ... as-saa:ah arba:ah.
Louis	tamaam, in sha'Allah.
Later on, Louis stops at a garage for petrol and asks for an oil-check.	
Louis	a:Tiini :ishriin laitir mumtaaz min faDHl-ak wa mumkin ti-chayyik al-aayil?

> **TIP**
> The term *four-wheel drive car*, or 4x4, can be expressed either as **foor-wiil** (*four-wheel*), or as **sayyaarah fii-ha dábal**.

2 Answer these questions.

a How does the clerk describe the car he is suggesting?

b What does he want to know about the car?

c How many days does Louis want the car for?

d How much is the rental for one day?

e Does the price include insurance?

f Which day and at what time must he return the car?

3 What is the Arabic for the following?
   a It's a very nice car!
   b One minute, please.
   c Saturday, at the same time.
   d When must I return it?

Language discovery

Find the Arabic expressions that mean:
   a twenty litres of premium
   b Can you check the oil?

LOAN WORDS DERIVED FROM ENGLISH

Gulf Arabic has adopted many words (mainly technical) from English. The plural of these words is usually formed by adding **-áat**, as shown in the brackets.

taayráat jadíidah *New tyres*

An unusual feature of Arabic grammar is that the feminine singular form of adjectives, in this case **jadiidah** (*new*), is used with non-human plural nouns.

áayil	*oil (for cars)*
ai-sii	*air-conditioning*
bánchar	*puncture*
biráik	*brakes*
lait (-áat)	*light (of a car)*
taayr (-áat)	*tyre(s)*
wárshah	*workshop*

Here are some more useful words you might need when driving in the Gulf.

banzíin	*petrol*
shíishah/maHáTTat banzíin	*petrol station*
:áadi	*ordinary, regular (petrol)*
mumtáaz	*super, premium (petrol)*
láitir, lítir (-áat)	*litre*
dáizil	*diesel*
kharbáan (adj.)	*broken down*

PRACTICE 2

Match the English to the Arabic.

a I'd like 25 litres of regular please.   1 as-sayyaarah maal-ti kharbaanah

b How much is a litre?   2 mumkin tichayyik at-taayraat?

c Can you check the tyres?   3 laitir bikam?

d Is there a workshop near here?   4 ariid khamsah w :ishriin laitir :aadi min faDHlak

e My car is broken down.   5 fiih warshah gariibah min hina?

Go further

READING ARABIC

Both **f** ف (**faa'**) and **q** ق (**qaaf**) look identical at the start and in the middle of a word, but **qaaf** on its own and at the end of a word has a looped tail below the line. Both have dots, one and two respectively. Note that **k** ك (**kaaf**) appears differently in every position.

faa'   ف

qaaf   ق

kaaf   ك

> **PRONUNCIATION TIP**
> Remember – the letter **q** (**qaaf**) is often pronounced as **g** in Gulf Arabic, so words such as **gahwah** and **gariib** are actually written with a **q** in Arabic script.

end of a word	middle of a word	start of a word	on its own
كيف؟	أدفع	فندق	ف
kaif?	**a-dfa:**	**funduq**	**faa'**
how?	*I pay*	hotel	
صديق	دقيقة	قارب	ق
Sadiiq	**daqiiqah**	**qaarib**	**qaaf**
friend	minute	boat	
بنك	سكر	كيلومتر	ك
bank	**sukkar**	**kiluumitir**	**kaaf**
bank	sugar	kilometre	

Look again at this Dubai road sign. Find the **qaaf** in the Arabic word for the place name **Al Quoz**, and the **faa'** in the word **Al Safa**.

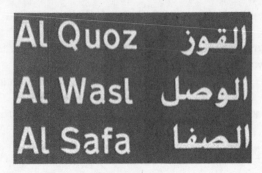

Identify the sign that says:
a cinema parking (**mawaaqif as-siinima**)
b Burj Khalifah
c sugar-free (**biduun sukkar**)
d cycle park (**saykil bark**)

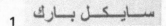

1 سـايــكــل بـارك

2 بدون سكر

3 برج خليفة

4 مواقف السينما

PRONUNCIATION TIP

As there is no letter *p* in Arabic, foreign words translated into Arabic script usually use the letter **baa'** instead, so *park* becomes **bark**. Likewise, **f** is used instead of **v**, so *video* becomes **fiidiyoo**.

How would you say these phrases in Arabic? The first word has been given to remind you how each phrase starts.

   a Is there a bus which goes to Abu Dhabi? fiih _____?
   b When does it arrive? mata _____?
   c How much is a single ticket? tadhkarat _____?
   d Give me a return ticket please. a:Tiini _____
   e I want to hire a car please. ariid _____
   f How much is the rental for one week? kam _____?
   g Can I pay by card? mumkin _____?

SELF CHECK

I CAN...
... book and buy travel tickets.
... hire a car.
... buy petrol and deal with basic car problems.

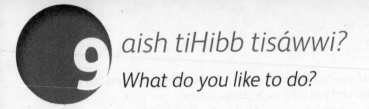

9 aish tiHibb tisáwwi?

What do you like to do?

In this unit you will learn how to:

▶ talk about what you do in your free time.
▶ say what you will do and when.
▶ say how often you do things.
▶ make arrangements to meet people.

CEFR: (A2) Can make arrangements to meet, decide where to go and what to do next. Can understand every day signs and notices in public places.

Leisure

You are sure to find lots of ways to spend your **wagt al-faráagh** (*free time*) in the Arabian Peninsula. Contrary to popular belief, it's not all **rimáal** (*sand dunes*), although there certainly are plenty of those! Weekends can be filled with water sports such as **as-sibáaHah** (*swimming*) or **al-ghooS** (*diving*). Walking in the **jibáal** (*mountains*) or along a **wáadi** (*valley* or *dry river bed*) is also popular and you are very likely to see families having a **jálsah** (*sitting together, perhaps with a picnic*).

When it comes to **ar-riyáaDhah** (*sport*), **kúrah** (*football*) is especially popular with Arabs, and many groups of friends play a game **:ála l-báHar**. If you have a **foor-wiil**, the desert is a great place for **at-takháyyam** (*camping*) with **aSdigáa'** (*friends*). Dune-bashing across the huge, rolling **rimáal** is a favourite pastime, but if you prefer to escape the heat for a while there is always plenty to do at the mall – **at-tasáwwag** (*shopping*), **as-síinima**. In Dubai you can even try **at-tazálluj** (*skiing*)!

 Someone asks you **tiHibb al-kurah?** What are they asking you?

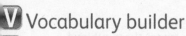

09.01 First look at these words and phrases, then complete them by adding the missing English words. Now listen and repeat.

wagt (waqt) al-faráagh	*free time*
Sayd as-sámak	*fishing*
ar-riyáaDHah	*sport*
al-musíiga	_____
as-sibáaHah	*swimming*
al-ghooS	*diving*
at-takháyyam	*camping*
ál:ab ...	*I play ...*
... kúrah	*... football*
... tánis	*... tennis*
... skwaash	*... _____*
arúuH ...	*I go (to) ...*
... as-suug	*... shopping*
... al-jábal (jibáal)	*... the mountain(s)*
... al-wáadi	*... the wadi (a usually dry valley or river bed)*
... aS-SaHaráa'	*... the desert*
... al-báH(a)r	*... the sea (also beach)*
... as-síinima	*... the _____*
asáwwi ...	*I do, make*
... ríHlah	*... a trip*
... jálsah	*... a gathering*
ashúuf at-tilifizyóon	*I watch _____*
astámi: li l-musíiga	*I listen to music*
ágra (áqra)	*I read*
azúur aSdigáa'	*I visit friends (m)*
azúur Sadiigáat	*I visit friends (f)*

> **TIP**
>
> A **jálsah**, in the social sense, is a general term for a gathering with friends or family and can take the form of a picnic, a barbecue or just sitting around together somewhere pleasant such as a **jálsah :ala l-baHar, :ala l-waadi** or **:ala l-jabal**.

 **NEW EXPRESSIONS**

09.02 Listen to these expressions, then repeat them out loud.

wain tirúuH?	*Where are you going?*
tiríid tiiji má:na?	*Do you want to come with us?*
maa ál:ab kúrah ábadan	*I never play _____*
aish ti-Híbb ti-sáwwi ...	*What do you like to do ...*
... fii wagt al-faráagh?	*... in your free time?*
aHyáanan ál:ab skwaash	*I sometimes play squash*
ba:d ash-shúghul (or ad-dawáam)	*after work*
níjlis fi l-bait	*We stay/are staying (lit. sitting) at home*
fi l-bait	*at home*
laish maa nsáwwii ríHla li ...?	*Why don't we make a trip to ...?*
fíkrah wáajid Hálwah!	*Great idea!*

Hiwaar 1 *Conversation 1*

09.03 *Sultan and Karim are work colleagues chatting about what they do in their free time. First listen, then answer the question.*

1 Which sport does Karim like playing?

Sultan	ahlan ya kariim, kaif Haalak?
Karim	ahlan ya sulTaan, al-Hamdu li-l-laah. w inta?
Sultan	al-Hamdu li-l-laah. wain tiruuH?
Karim	aruuH al:ab kurah ma:a aSdigaa'-i. nal:ab marrtain fi l-usbuu: :ala l-baHar. tiriid tiiji ma:a?
Sultan	laa, shukran — maa aHibb al-kurah.
Karim	aish tiHibb tisawwi fii wagt al-faraagh?
Sultan	aHyaanan al:ab skwaash ba:d ash-shughul.

They go on to talk about their plans for the weekend.

Karim	aish bitsawwi yoom al-khamiis?
Sultan	maa a:raf ... mumkin binijlis fi l-bait, nshuuf at-tilifizyoon.
Karim	laish maa nsawwi riHlah li Suur ma:a al-awlaad?
Sultan	fikrah waajid Hálwah! mumkin nsawwi jalsah :ala baHar.
Karim	Tayyib, nruuH yoom al-khamiis fi S-SubaH, ya:ani ... as-saa:ah tis:ah?
Sultan	tamáam, bashuufak yoom al-khamiis as-saa:ah tis:ah, in shaa' Al-láah.

09.03 Listen again and this time speak Karim's part.

2 What is the correct answer?

a Karim plays football …

1 once a week   2 twice a week   3 three times a week

b Sultan plays squash …

1 on Saturday   2 before work   3 after work

c They are planning a trip to …

1 the beach   2 the cinema   3 the mall

3 Match the English to the Arabic.

a Maybe we'll stay at home.   **1** bashuufak yoom al-khamíis.

b Great idea.   **2** aruuH al:ab kurah.

c I'll see you Thursday.   **3** tiriid tiiji ma:na?

d I'm going to play football.   **4** mumkin nijlis fi l-bait.

e Do you want to come with us?   **5** fikrah waajid Halwah

4 Are these statements true or false?

a Karim plays football with his brother.

b Sultan also likes football.

c They are going to take the children on the trip.

d They are planning to go on Friday.

 Language discovery

 **What is the Arabic for the words in bold?**

a I play **twice a week**.   **d** Maybe **we will stay at home**.

b **Sometimes** I play squash.   **e** **I will see you** on Thursday.

c **I'm going to play** football.

1 SAYING HOW OFTEN YOU DO THINGS

 09.04 Here are some phrases you will find useful.

aHyáanan	*sometimes*
dáayman	*always*
kill *or* **kull yoom**	*every day*
márrah/marr(a)táin ...	*once/twice ...*
thaláath marráat ...	*three times ...*
... fi l-yoom	*... a day*
... fi l-usbúu:	*... a week*
... fi sh-sháhar	*... a month*
... fi s-sánah	*... a year*

al-Hiin dáwr-ak! *Now your turn!*

Complete each sentence by adding the correct Arabic.

a	_____al:ab tanis.	*I sometimes play tennis.*
b	aruuH al-mool_____yoom.	*I go to the mall every day.*
c	al:ab kurah_____fi l-usbuu:.	*I play football once a week.*
d	_____anaam ba:d al-ghada'.	*I always sleep after lunch.*
e	daayman amshi _____al-:ásha.	*I always walk after dinner.*

> **OMANI SAYING**
>
> In Oman they have a helpful saying: **tghádda w tsádda, t:áshsha w tmáshsha**, which translates as *Have lunch, then sleep, have dinner, then walk.*

> **ABADAN**
>
> Use the negative adverb **abadan** in conjunction with **maa** (*not*).
> **maa arúuH al-mool ábadan.**   *I never go to the mall.*
>
> If you want to really emphasize *never*, lengthen the last **a** on **abadan**:
> **maa arúuH al-baHar abadáan!**   *I never go to the sea!*

2 SAYING WHAT YOU WILL DO IN THE FUTURE

Spoken Arabic in the Gulf expresses the future by adding the letter **b-** to the present tense form of the verb. A helping vowel, usually **-i**, is added before a consonant. The vowels of the present tense prefixes are left out to smooth the pronunciation.

barúuH	I will go	binrúuH	we will go
bitrúuH	you will go (m)	bitruuHúun	you will go (pl)
bitruuHíin	you will go (f)	biyruuHúun	they will go
biyrúuH	he will go		
bitrúuH	she will go		

PRACTICE 1

1 Match these sports to the correct Arabic word.

   a booling   **b** airoobik   **c** kurah

   d at-tazalluj :ala l-maay   **e** ghooS   **f** at-tazalluj :ala th-thalj

   g Sayd as-samak   **h** goolf   **I** tanis aT-Taawilah

TIP	
at-tazalluj :ala l-maay	water-skiing
at-tazalluj :ala th-thalj	ice-skating, also skiing

2 Match the English to the Arabic.

a	sometimes	1	maa … abadan
b	always	2	marrah fi l-usbuu:
c	never	3	aHyaanan
d	once a week	4	ba:d al-ghada'
e	every day	5	daayman
f	after lunch	6	kull yoom

 Now cover up the Arabic and say the phrases out loud.

3 Match the Arabic and English forms of the future verb *will go.*

a	you (f) will go	1	baruuH
b	we will go	2	biyruuH
c	she will go	3	bitruuHiin
d	he will go	4	binruuH
e	I will go	5	bitruuH

4 Match the English to the Arabic, then select the correct future verb form.

a	She will go to Riyadh on Friday.	1	basawwi/binsawwi jalsah :ala l-baHar
b	He will go to the mall after work.	2	bashuuf/binshuuf at-tilifizyoon ba:d aDH-DHuhr
c	I will watch TV in the afternoon.	3	biyruuH/bitruuH al-mool ba:d ash-shughal
d	We will have a BBQ on the beach.	4	baruuH/bitruuH ar-riyaaDH yoom al-jum:ah

🎧 Listen and understand

1 09.05 **Listen to each speaker talk about their leisure time, then say what activity each person does and when or how often they do it.**

	Activity?	When/how often?
a		
b		
c		
d		
e		

2 09.06 Salim is interviewing Fatima about what she likes to do in her free time. Which of the ten expressions listed do you hear as they talk? Listen to the conversation as many times as you need.

sometimes	cinema
sport	shopping
music	swimming
inshaa'Al-laah	with my friends
I read	I don't like

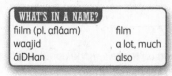

> **WHAT'S IN A NAME?**
> fiilm (pl. afláam)   film
> waajid   a lot, much
> áiDHan   also

3 Match each question to its correct answer.

a aish tisawwi fii wagt al-faraagh?   **1** na:am, al:ab kurah kull yoom

b aish tiriid tisawwi yoom al-khamiis?   **2** ya:ani … marrtain fi sh-shahar

c tiHibb ar-riyaaDHah?   **3** baruuH al-baHar in shaa' Al-laah

d tiruuH as-siinima waajid?   **4** ariid aruuH al-maT:am

e wain bitruuH yoom al-sabt?   **5** al:ab tanis wa skwaash

 4 How would you answer the questions in the previous exercise yourself?

 NEW EXPRESSIONS

09.07 Add the missing English word to complete the phrase, then listen and repeat.

báachir/báakir/búkrah	tomorrow
mashghúul/mashghúulah	busy (m/f)
fáaDHi/fáaDHiyah	free
aish al-barnáamij?	What's the plan (of activity)?
ayy makáan	anywhere
aish rá'y-ak?	What do you think? (m)
aish rá'y-ich?	What _____? (f)

áasif/áasifah	*(I'm) sorry (m/f)*
ba:d báakir	*(the day) after _____*
múmkin nruuH nzuur ...	*We could go and visit ...*
munáasib/munáasibah	*suitable, convenient (m/f)*
as-sáa:ah khámsah munáasibah l-ich?	*Is five o'clock convenient for you? (f)*

al-Hiin dáwr-ak! *Now your turn!*

Ask your brother if it would be convenient for him to meet you at five o'clock.

🐪 Hiwáar 2 *Conversation 2*

09.08 *Fatima is talking to her friend Samira on the telephone about what to do on their day off. First listen, then answer the question.*

1 Where do Fatima and Samira decide to go?

Fatima	inti mashghuulah baakir?
Samira	laa, ana faaDHiyah. aish al-barnaamij?
Fatima	maa a:raf. wain tiriidiin tiruuHiin?
Samira	ayy makaan ... aish ra'y-ich?
Fatima	tiriidiin tiruuHiin al-mool?
Samira	laa aasifah, baruuH ba:d baakir in shaa'Al-laah ma:a ukhti.
Fatima	mumkin nruuH nzuur salma wa shamsah?
Samira	tamaam. nruuH as-saa:ah kam?
Fatima	as-saa:ah a:sharah munaasibah l-ich?
Samira	aywa. ashuuf-ich baakir in shaa'Al-laah.
Fatima	in shaa'Al-laah.

2 Answer the following questions:
   a What does Fatima first suggest?
   b Why doesn't Samira want to go?
   c Where do they decide to go?
   d What time do they decide to go?

Language discovery

Find the expressions in the dialogue that mean:
a Where do you want to go?
b Do you want to go to the mall?
c We could go and visit Salma and Shamsa.

VERB STRINGS (I'M GOING TO ... + VERB)

In English we can express future plans or intention by saying *I'm going to* + another verb, as in *I'm going to talk to him tomorrow*. But Arabic doesn't have an infinitive form, so you just keep adding the same form of the verb to your string.

aish tiruuHti sawwi?	*What are you going to do?* *(What you-go you-do?)*
aruuH ashuuf (fiilm)	*I'm going to see (a film)*
aruuH azuur	*I'm going to visit (I-go I-visit)*
aruuH al:ab	*I'm going to play (I-go I-play)*
aruuH at:allam	*I'm going to learn (I-go I-learn)*
aruuH asawwi	*I'm going to do/make (I-go I-do/make)*

PRACTICE 2

1 **Rearrange the Arabic to make sentences given in English below. Then say the sentences out loud.**

a s-siinima   ashuuf   fi   fiilm   aruuH
I'm going to see a film in the cinema.

b amshi   l-baHar   aruuH   :ala
I'm going to walk on the beach.

c sidaab   aruuH   ahl-i   azuur   fii
I'm going to visit my family in Sidab.

d aruuH   Sadiig-i   al:ab   ma:a   goolf
I'm going to play golf with my friend.

e agra'   fi   aruuH   l-Hadiiqah
I'm going to read in the garden.

f al-lughah   at:allam   al-yabaaniyyah   aruuH.
I'm going to learn Japanese.

2 How would you answer these questions yourself?

aish tiruuH tisawwi ...

   a baakir?
   b yoom as-sabt?
   c al-usbuu: al-gaadim (next week)?

Go further

 READING ARABIC

In this unit you will learn how to read the letters **l** ل (**laam**), **m** م (**miim**), **h** ه (**haa'**) and **w** و (**waaw**). You have already met **laam** in Unit 1 when you learnt **alif-laam**, but it is useful to know how it appears in different positions. **miim** is a ball and looks very similar in all its positions. **haa'** looks quite different in each position – try to learn each one. **waaw** looks exactly the same in each position but doesn't join to any letter after it.

end of a word	middle of a word	start of a word	on its own
جبل **jabal** *mountain*	رحلة **riHlah** *trip*	ليمون **laimoon** *lemon*	ل **laam**
كم **kam?** *how much?*	خمسة **khamsah** *five*	مول **mool** *mall*	م **miim**
وجه **wajh** *face*	قهوة **qahwah** *coffee*	هذا **haadha** *this (m)*	ه **haa'**
راديو **raadyo** *radio*	غوص **ghooS** *diving*	وادي **waadi** *valley/river bed*	و **waaw**

1 The letters laam, miim, haa' and waaw appear in each of these common signs and labels. Using the table, identify which of these letters appear in each word. Some letters appear more than once in the same word!

Example: a laam and ....

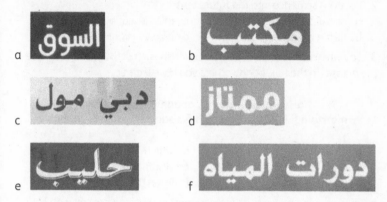

a السوق

b مكتب

c دبي مول

d ممتاز

e حليب

f دورات المياه

2 09.09 Now match up each Arabic sign in Exercise 1 to its pronunciation.

> Haliib   dooraat al-miyaah (*bathrooms*)
> dubay mool   as-suug   maktab (*office*) · mumtaaz (*super*)

3 Listen to the pronunciation of each word then repeat.

Test yourself

 1 In Arabic tell a friend whether you like or dislike these activities.

  a scuba diving   **c** swimming

  b sport   **d** camping

2 Put each sentence into the future tense.

  a ana al:ab kurah   **c** inta tishuuf at-tilifizyoon

  b niHna nal:ab skwaash   **d** huwwa yiruuH al-mool

 3 Say when or how often you participate in each activity. You could use the phrases in the box, or any others you have learned.

> **aHyaanan   maa ... abadan   kull yoom**
> **marrtain fi l-usbuu: marrah fi s-sanah   yoom al-jum:ah**

  a play tennis   **d** watch TV

  b go to the cinema   **e** visit friends

  c go the beach   **f** listen to music

 4 Following the prompts, speak your part in the conversation with Faris.

Faris	inta mashghoul baakir?
inta	*Say no, you're free.*
Faris	aish al-barnaamij
inta	*We could play football on the beach.*
Faris	nzain. as-saa:ah kam nruuH?
inta	*Say five o'clock.*
Faris	nzain.
inta	*Say you will hopefully see him tomorrow.*
Faris	in in shaa' Allah. ma:a as-salaamah.
inta	*Say goodbye.*

SELF CHECK

	I CAN. . .
○	... talk about what I do in my free time.
○	... say what I will do.
○	... say how often I do things.
○	... make arrangements to meet people.

10 li-wain ruHt fi l-ijáazah?

Where did you go on holiday?

In this unit you will learn how to:
▶ *say the months of the year.*
▶ *talk about your last holiday.*
▶ *say what you have done.*
▶ *describe the weather.*

CEFR: (A2) *Can communicate in simple and routine tasks requiring a simple and direct exchange of information on familiar topics and activities. Can describe past activities and personal experiences.*

Holiday time

Gulf countries observe a number of special Islamic holidays, such as **:iid** (*Eid*) **al-fitr**, a three-day celebration marking the end of the fasting period during Ramadan. At such times roads can get busy and flights and hotels booked up as people make the most of their time off work to spend with friends and family away from home. Of course, weather can be a key factor in deciding when and where to go on holiday. In the Gulf, **al-jaww** (*the weather*) varies from region to region, but in general things can get **wáajid Haarr** (*very hot*) **fi S-Saif** (*in the summer*) and the **dárajat il-Haráarah** (*temperature*) can soar well above 40°C **min máayo li sabtámbar**. Despite the heat, there are countless places to visit during **ijáazat aS-Saif**. You could travel **bi T-Tayyáarah** (*by plane*) to somewhere a little cooler such as the city of Salalah in the south of Oman. During **ash-shíta** (*the winter*), however, temperatures are generally much more pleasant with just a small chance of **máTar** (*rain*) or even **thalj** (*snow*) high up in the **jábal**.

Find the Arabic for:
a   from May to September
b   the summer holiday

128

Vocabulary builder

 10.01 First add the missing English words, then listen and repeat the Arabic out loud.

SHUHÚUR AS-SÁNAH	MONTHS OF THE YEAR
yanáayir	January
fibráayir	February
mars	March
abríil	_____
máayo	May
yúunyo	June
yúulyo	July
aghúsTos	_____
sabtámbar	September
októobar	October
nufámbar	November
disámbar	_____
fii yanáayir	in January
fii abríil	in April
fi S-Saif	in the summer
fi sh-shíta	in the winter

NEW EXPRESSIONS

 10.02 Add the missing English words, then listen and repeat the Arabic out loud.

as-sánah l-máaDHiyah	last _____
ruHt hináak min gábil?	Have you (m) been there before?
kaan	was (m)
káanat	was (f)
áwwal márrah	the _____ time
áwwalan	firstly, first of all
sáafart	I travelled
sáafarna	_____ travelled
ruHt	I went
rúHna	we went
zurt	_____ visited
zúrna	we visited
kaif sáafartu?	How did you (pl) travel?

bi T-Tayyáarah	by _____
bi s-sayyáarah	by _____
aish sawwáitu?	What did you (pl) do?
sawwáina ríHlah	we went on a trip (lit. we made a trip)
shuft Huut	_____ saw a whale
shúfna Huut	we saw a whale
ishtaráit	I bought
ishtaráina	_____ bought
min sanatáin	two years ago
waalidáin	parents
biláad(f) (buldáan pl)	country
sámak (pl. asmáak)	fish
ashyáa' kathíirah	many things
mumtáaz/mumtáazah	excellent (m)

Hiwaar 1 *Conversation 1*

10.03 *Saif asks Oliver about where he went on his last holiday. First listen, then answer the question.*

1 Which two countries did Oliver visit?

Saif	li-wain ruHtu fi l-ijaazah?
Oliver	as-sanah l-maaDHiyah ruHt al-imaaraat w :umaan ma:a waalidayy.
Saif	:umaan bilaad waajid jamiilah. ruHt hinaak min gabil?
Oliver	laa, kaanat haadhi awwal marrah. inta ta:raf :umaan?
Saif	na:am. ruHt hinaak min sanatain. kaif saafartu?
Oliver	awwalan saafarna min landan li-dubay bi T-Tayyaarah wa ba:dain ruHna masqaT bi s-sayyaarah. kaanat riHlah waajid Tawiilah laakin masqaT madiinah jamiilah.
Saif	aish sawwaitu fii masqaT?
Oliver	zurna suug as-samak wa suug adh-dhahab. sawwaina riHlah li l-baHar w shufna Huut w asmaak kathiirah.
Saif	w aish sawwaitu fi l-imaaraat?
Oliver	zurna mataaHif kathiirah fi sh-sharjah wa shufna burj khaliifah fii dubay. fii aakhir yoom zurt al-mool w ishtarait ashyaa' kathiirah. kaanat ijaazah mumtaazah.
Saif	maa shaa' Al-laah!

10.03 Listen again, and this time speak the part of Oliver.

> **BEWARE THE WADI!**
>
> Rainy days are few and far between in most parts of the Gulf, so when it rains, it is quite an event! As the ground is usually so dry, a **wadi** can fill up very quickly and become dangerous to cross, so be careful or you might find yourself stranded on one side for several hours!

2 Match the Arabic to the correct English.

a li-wain ruHt fi l-ijaazah?

b kaanat riHlah waajid Tawiilah.

c zurna suug as-samak.

d aish sawwaitu fi l-imaaraat?

e ishtarait ashyaa' kathiirah.

1 It was a long journey.

2 What did you do in the Emirates?

3 I bought many things.

4 We visited the fish market.

5 Where did you go during the holidays?

3 Are these statements true or false?

a Oliver went to Muscat by car.

b They made a trip to the mountains.

c They visited the museum in Muscat.

d On the last day he went to the shopping mall.

4 Listen to the conversation again, then choose the correct answers.

a When did Oliver go on holiday?

i last week

ii last month

iii last year

iv two years ago

b This was his _____ visit to Oman.

i first

ii second

iii third

iv fourth

c Where <u>didn't</u> they go?

i to the shops

ii to the beach

iii to the museum

iv to the wadi

Language discovery

Say out loud the Arabic for each expression in bold.

a Last year **I went** to Oman.

b **We saw** a whale and a lot of fish.

c **We made** a trip to the beach.

d **I visited** the shopping mall.

10 *li-wain ruHt fi l-ijáazah? Where did you go on holiday?* **131**

With most Arabic verbs the past tense is formed by adding an ending (or suffix) to the past stem. There are no prefixes, only suffixes. There is no word in Arabic like English *to go*; instead, the Arabs use the past tense he-form, which is the simplest, with no suffix, and this is the past stem.

> **TIP**
> There are four types of verb in Arabic, but don't worry too much about this now. At this stage you can just use these tables for reference.

Many verbs have just one past stem, like **katab** (*he wrote*).

Singular	Meaning	Plural	Meaning
katáb-t	*I wrote*	katáb-na	*we wrote*
katáb-t	*you wrote* (m)	katáb-tu	*you wrote* (pl)
katáb-ti	*you wrote* (f)		
kátab	*he wrote*	kátab-u	*they wrote*
kátab-at	*she wrote*		

1 Here are the past stems of some more verbs you have learned that follow the same pattern as katab in the past tense.

Past stem	Meaning
la:b	*played*
sáafar	*travelled*
rája:	*returned*
takállam	*spoke*
ishtághal	*worked*
sábaH	*swam*
shárab	*drank*

al-Hiin dáwr-ak! *Now your turn!*

   a Put each verb in the table into the past tense *I*-form, e.g.
      la:bt *I played*.

   b Put each verb into the past tense *we*-form, e.g. **la:bna** *we played*.

2 Some verbs have two past stems, such as **ruH/raaH** (*go*). Only the *he-*, *she-* and *they*-forms use the **raaH**-stem. All other forms use the **ruH**-stem.

Singular	Meaning	Plural	Meaning
ruH-t	*I went*	rúH-na	*we went*
ruH-t	*you went* (m)	rúH-tu	*you went* (pl)
rúH-ti	*you went* (f)		
raaH	*he went*	ráaH-u	*they went*
ráaH-at	*she went*		

Here are some common verbs with two past tense stems. In each pair the *he-/she-/they*-stem is given second, as in **ruH/raaH**. The present stem has also been given to help you recognize verbs you have already met in previous units.

Past stem	Present stem	Meaning
ruH/raaH	ruuH	*go*
nim/naam	naam	*sleep*
zur/zaar	zuur	*visit*
shuf/shaaf	shuuf	*see*

There are other verbs with two past stems but which work in a slightly different way, e.g. *do* or *make*.

Past stem	Meaning	Past stem	Meaning
sawwái-t	*I did, made*	sawwái-na	*we did, made*
sawwái-t	*you (m) did, made*	sawwái-tu	*you (pl) did, made*
sawwái-ti	*you (f) did, made*		
sáww-a	*he did, made*	sáww-u	*they did, made*
sáww-at	*she did, made*		

The verbs **ishtarai/ishtar** (*buy*), **mashai/mash** (*walk*) and **garai/gara** (*read*) work in the same way.

For more details of the past tense, see *Complete Arabic* and *Complete Spoken Arabic*.

 PRACTICE 1

1 Match the Arabic to the correct English.
   a al-usbuu: al-maaDHi   1 last year
   b ash-shahr al-maaDHi   2 last week
   c as-sanah al-maaDHiyah   3 last month

2 Match the Arabic to the correct English.
   a ruHt   1 I visited
   b sawwait   2 I drank
   c ishtarait   3 I went
   d zurt   4 I did, made
   e shuft   5 I bought
   f sharabt   6 I saw

3 Change the present to the past tense, then say each sentence. Begin each sentence with *ams* (*yesterday*).

a ana aruuH as-siinima.

b huwwa yishrab gahwah.

c niHna nizuur al-matHaf.

d inti tiruuHiin al-mool.

e huwwa yishtaghal fi l-maktab.

f humma yiruuHuun suug adh-dhahab.

TIP

Pronouns have been given to help you, but remember that pronouns are optional when speaking Arabic.

---

4 Now translate your answers into English.

5 Here is Fatima's email to her friend Samia in Baghdad. Are the statements following true (T), false (F), or not in text (NT)?

:aziizati saamiya,

kaif Haal-ich w aish akhbaar-ich? ash-shahr al-maaDHi ana ruHt al-baHrain ma:a ukhti :azza. zurna qal:at al-baHrain w mool kabiir ismuh 'baHrain siti santar'. hinaak ishtarait kutub kathiirah w ukhti ishtarat malaabis jadidah. aHibb as-safar!

akhi aHmad yiskun fii dubay wa yizuur abu DHabi waajid. al-usbuu: al-maaDhi zaar jaami: ash-shaikh zaayid al-kabiir ma:a aSdigaa min faransa. al-jaami: waajid jamiil w kabiir! Sadiigati sharloot raaHat dubay gabil shahr w zaarat Hadiigat al-maaya. inti ruHti dubay min gabil?

faaTimah ☺

TIP

aziizati	*(my) dear* (f)	akhbáar	*news*
kitáab (kútub)	*book(s)*	maláabis	*clothes*
jaami:	*large mosque*	qál:ah	*fort*

---

a Fatima visited Bahrain with her brother.

b Fatima bought new clothes.

c Her brother lives in Dubai.

d Her brother is an engineer.

e Fatimah visited Sheikh Zayed Grand Mosque.

f Her friend Charlotte visited Dubai last year.

g Her brother visited a water park.

6 Where a statement is false, give the true statement in English.

 7 Now imagine that the email was sent to you. Reply in Arabic, saying where you went on your last holiday and three activities you did.

8 10.04 What happened on Friday? Listen to each person and list their activities in English.

	morning	afternoon
a		
b		
c		
d		

 9 *aish sawwait ams? What did you do yesterday?* Complete the phrases with your own activities in the past tense.

a ams *(yesterday)*

b al-khamiis al-maaDHi *(last Thursday)*

c ash-shahar al-maaDHi *(last month)*

d as-sanah al-maaDHiyah? *(last year)*

NEW EXPRESSIONS

10.05 **Listen, then repeat out loud.**

al-jaww	*the weather*
al-jaww zain	*the weather is good*
al-jaww muu zain	*the weather is not good*
al-jaww báarid (adj)	*the weather is cold*
al-jaww Haarr (adj)	*the weather is hot*
fiih ...	*it's ... [lit. there is]*
... shams	*... sunny (lit. there is sun)*
... ghaim	*... cloudy (lit. there are clouds)*
... háwa	*... windy (lit. there is wind)*
... máTar	*... raining (lit. there is rain)*
... thalj	*... snowing (lit. there is snow)*
dárajat il-Haráarah thalathíin	*it is 30°C (degree the-heat (is) 30)*
móosam aS-Saif	*the season (of) summer*
móosam ash-shíta	*the season (of) winter*

Now cover up the Arabic and repeat out loud.

Instead of **al-jaww báarid/Haarr** you can use:

fiih bard (noun)	*it is cold* (lit. *there is cold*)
fiih Harr (noun)	*it is hot* (lit. *there is heat*)

 Hiwáar 2 *Conversation 2*

10.06 Robin is asking Khamis about his business trip to Australia last month. First listen, then answer the questions below.

Robin	kaif kaan al-jaww fii sidni?
Khamis	al-usbuu: al-awwal kaan al-jaww Haarr, laakin al-usbuu: ath-thaani kaan fiih bard w maTar w hawa shwayya.
Robin	ya khaSaarah! fii yanaayir?
Khamis	aywa, al-Hiin móosam aS-Saif fii ustraaliya.
Robin	saHiiH.
Khamis	inta ruHt ustraaliya min gabil?
Robin	laa abadan, ustraaliya waajid ba:iidah :an ingilterra! ruHt ayy makaan ghair hinaak?
Khamis	aywa, :indi Sadiig gariib min brizban. ruHt bi T-Tayaarah - brizban ba:iidah :an sidni! kunt fii brisban yoomain bass.

> **TIP**
> **saHiiH** *true* **khaSáarah** *shame, pity*

1 Match the Arabic to the English.

a	kaan fiih bard w maTar	**1**	How was the weather?
b	brizban ba:iidah :an sidni	**2**	It was cold and it rained.
c	ruHt bi T-Tayaarah	**3**	Did you go anywhere else?
d	kaif kaan al-jaww?	**4**	I went by plane.
e	ruHt ayy makaan ghair?	**5**	Brisbane is far from Sydney.

2 When was Khamis in Sydney?

a	January	**b**	April	**c**	July

3 How many times has Robin been to Australia?

a	once	**b**	twice	**c**	never

4 For how long was Khamis in Brisbane?
  a one day   **b** two days   **c** a week

5 Find the Arabic for:
  a The weather was hot.
  b It was cold and it rained.
  c I was in Brisbane for just two days.

Language discovery

1 KAAN

In Arabic no verb is used for *is/are*, but the verb **kaan** means *was/were*.
Here is another verb with two past tense stems!

Singular	Meaning	Plural	Meaning
kun-t	*I was*	**kún-na**	*we were*
kun-t	*you were* (m)	**kún-tu**	*you were* (pl)
kún-ti	*you were* (f)		
kaan	*he was*	**káan-u**	*they were*
káan-at	*she was*		

> **TIP**
>
> **kaan** has a present tense form **yikúun**, but **yikúun** can also imply a future or potential event. For further details, see *Complete Arabic* and *Complete Spoken Arabic*.

NEW EXPRESSIONS

 10.07 Listen and repeat out loud.

kunt fii madiinat al-kuwait as-sabt al-maaDHi.	*I was in Kuwait city last Saturday.*
kaan al-jaww baarid.	*The weather was cold.*
ams kunna fi l-mool.	*Yesterday we were in the mall.*
kaan fiih masbaH fi l-fundug.	*There was a pool in the hotel.*
kaan :indi foor-wiil fii dubay.	*I had a 4x4 in Dubai.*

> **TIP**
>
> To make **kaan** negative, just add **maa** before it. For example:
> **maa kaan fiih shams.**   *It wasn't sunny.*
> **maa kaan :indi wagt.**   *I didn't have time.*

al-Hiin dáwr-ak! *Now your turn!*

Say each sentence out loud in Arabic. Start with the correct form of kaan.

a I was in Doha last week.

b The restaurant was closed on Friday.

c The film was very good.

d He had a big house in London.

e There were a lot of people in the market yesterday.

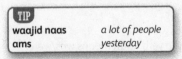

TIP	
waajid naas	*a lot of people*
ams	*yesterday*

2 SAYING HOW THE WEATHER WAS IN THE PAST

To talk about the weather in the past tense, just add **kaan** to the beginning of the phrase.

▶ **al-jaww zain → kaan al-jaww zain**

▶ **fiih maTar → kaan fiih maTar**

kaan fiih Haar, wa kaanat darajat il-Haraarah arba:iin.

It was hot, and the temperature (f) was 40°C.

PRACTICE 2

1 Match the Arabic to the English.

a	The weather is cold.	**1**	al-jaww muu zain
b	It is raining.	**2**	fiih thalj
c	It is hot.	**3**	al-jaww baarid
d	The weather is not good.	**4**	al-jaww zain
e	It is snowing.	**5**	fiih Harr
f	The weather is nice.	**6**	fiih maTar

2 Now say each Arabic phrase using the past tense.

3 Match the Arabic to the English.

a	kaan	**1**	she was
b	kunna	**2**	you were (fem. sing)
c	kaanat	**3**	he was
d	kaanu	**4**	we were
e	kunt	**5**	they were
f	kunti	**6**	I was

138

Go further

READING ARABIC

Congratulations on reaching Unit 10 of Reading Arabic! You have completed the hardest part by learning all the letters of the Arabic alphabet in their different positions, so now you can begin to read some simple sentences in Arabic.

One of the more challenging aspects of reading Arabic is that usually only the long vowels are shown in the script. Thus, the written word **kitaab** (*book*), would look like **k-t-aa-b**. The **i** sound after the **k** is not written so how can you tell if the letter **k** is pronounced **ka**, **ku**, **ki**, or simply **k**? In this final part of Reading Arabic we introduce you to the short vowels (**a-i-u**), the doubling symbol (**sháddah**) and the zero-vowel symbol (**sukúun**).

Short vowels, sháddah and sukúun

Short vowel symbols are added above and below Arabic letters to help you recognize how to pronounce those letters. Note that in Arabic there is no *e* or *o* vowel.

The short vowel symbols are:

a – a small dash above the letter (known as **fátHah**) as in the **ba**-sound بَ in **bank** (*bank*) بَنك

i – a small dash below the letter (known as **kásrah**) as in the ki-sound كِ in **kitáab** (*book*) كِتاب

u – a mini letter **waaw** symbol above the letter (known as **Dámmah**), as in the du-sound دُ in **dukkáan** (*shop*) دُكان

Two additional symbols which are useful to recognise to help you read and pronounce a word accurately are:

sháddah, which shows where a letter is doubled e.g. in the word سيّارة **sayyáarah** (*car*) a **sháadah** is placed above the letter **yaa'** يّ to indicate the doubled **yy** sound.

sukúun, which shows that there is no vowel sound at all after the main sound of the letter, as in the **k** ك in مَكْتب (*office*).

> **TIP**
>
> A **shadda** looks like a little, curvy English letter *w* above the letter that is doubled, and a **sukkuun** looks like a little *zero*.

You will have noticed that none of the words introduced in Arabic script so far, including the photos of signs and labels, have shown these symbols.

This is quite normal in Arabic. But many Arabic students' books show them in the Arabic script, so it is very useful to understand what they mean once you begin to advance your Arabic to the next level.

1 In each sentence, identify the Arabic word that matches its English description. Read from right to left.

a	Something to eat?	أنا أحب السمك
b	Something to drink?	أشرب القهوة كل يوم
c	A method of transport?	سافرت إلى دبي بالسيارة
d	A day of the week?	المطعم مفتوح كل يوم سبت

2 What do the words you have identified mean in English?

a _____   b _____

c _____   d _____

3 10.08 Now read out loud each sentence in Arabic written with the short vowels, shadda and sukuun marked where appropriate. Remember to read from right to left.

| a أَنَا أُحِبُّ السَّمَكَ |
| b أَشْرَبُ الْقَهْوَةَ كُلَّ يَوْمْ |
| c سَافَرْتُ إِلَى دُبَي بِالسَّيَارَة |
| d الْمَطْعَمْ مَفْتُوحْ كُلَّ يُومْ سبت |

PRONUNCIATION

Remember that the **laam** in **alif-laam** is not pronounced before a Sun letter!

TIP

As explained in the introduction, the spoken Arabic you hear and the written Arabic you see may not always use exactly the same form because written Arabic is not usually spoken, and vice versa, but don't worry about this – this is quite usual all over the Arab world and you will get used to it as your Arabic improves. At this stage, whenever you come across Arabic, whether written or spoken, just listen or watch out for key words and phrases you recognize to help you get started.

4 What does each sentence mean in English?

Mastering the short vowels, **shaddah** and **sukuun** symbols will help to accelerate your learning and ability to read Arabic script. It is not easy, but do stick at it – being able to understand Arabic script when you are out and about in the Gulf is one of the most rewarding aspects of learning Arabic. Develop your Arabic reading and writing skills further with *Complete Arabic*.

? Test yourself

1 Look at the pictures. In Arabic tell a friend what you did.

a

c

b

d

2 In Arabic tell your friend about your last holiday. You may wish to use some of the words/phrases in the box.

ruHt	**shuft**	**ishtarait**	**kaan**
bi s-sayyaarah	**ma:a**	**saafart**	**zurt**

a li-wain ruHt fi l-ijaazah? (*Where did you go on holiday?*)

b ma:a man? (*With whom?*)

c kaif saafart? (*How did you travel?*)

d aish sawwait? (*What did you do?*)

e kaif kaan al-jaww? (*How was the weather?*)

SELF CHECK

	I CAN...
○	... say the months of the year.
○	... talk about my last holiday.
○	... say what I have done.
○	... describe the weather.

Review: Units 7–10

1 **Match each place in town to its correct name in Arabic.**

a	bariid	**1**	police station
b	fundug	**2**	hospital
c	mustashfa	**3**	town centre
d	markaz ash-shurTah	**4**	fish market
e	suug as-samak	**5**	hotel
f	wasaT al-madiinah	**6**	post office

 2 **What do these people like doing? Read each statement out loud in Arabic, then give your answers in English.**

   a Fatima: ana aHibb aruuH as-siinima.

   b Ahmed: ana al:ab kurah.

   c Qaasim: ana aHibb as-sibaaHah w al-ghooS.

   d Faisal: ana maa aHibb al-kurah, afaDHDHal al:ab skwaash.

   e Laila: ana aHibb asawwi jalsah aw aruuH as-suug ma:a Sadiigaati.

   f Sara: ana maa aHibb ar-riyaaDHah. afaDHDHal al-musiiga, w ijlis fi l-bait, ashuuf at-tilifizyuun, kidha …

> **TIP**
> **kidha** *that sort of thing, like that*

 3 **Ask the way to these places in town. Remember to start with law samaHt or law samaHti (as appropriate).**

a	the beach (to a man)	**d**	airport (to a man)
b	the market (to a woman)	**e**	the bank (to a man)
c	the pharmacy (to a woman)	**f**	the supermarket (to a woman)

4 **What's the grammar rule here? Complete the sentence by adding the missing Arabic phrase.**

To say *there is/there* are you say _____, and to say *there isn't/aren't* you say _____.

5 **Match the Arabic to the correct direction in English, saying the Arabic out loud.**

a	liff yisaar	**1**	take the first right
b	khudhi awwal yamiin	**2**	at the roundabout
c	ruuH siidah	**3**	second right
d	ba:d ad-dawwaar	**4**	turn left
e	thaani yamiin	**5**	after the roundabout
f	:ind ad-dawwaar	**6**	go straight on

6 List the ordinal numbers in rank order from lowest to highest, saying them out loud in Arabic.

a thaalith	**d** thaani	**g** raabi:
b taasi:	**e** khaamis	**h** saadis
c saabi:	**f** thaamin	**i** awwal

7 Rearrange the Arabic letters to make six words/phrases relating to free time (wagt al-faraagh).

a auhkr

b hljaas

c Hashaaib

d isimagu

e nisamii

f Hrau la-lomo

8 Rearrange these Arabic words to make five statements about al-jaww, then say the completed statements out loud.

a zain   al-yoom   al-jaww

b fi   al-jaww   l-baHrain   kaif?

c al-jaww   baarid   kaan

d maTar   aS-SubaH   fiih   kaan

e wa   il-Haraarah   thalaathiin   sittah   darajat

9 Which is the odd one out in each case?

a baarid   shams   thalj   falaafil

b bi T-Tayyaarah   bi-sukkar   bi s-sayyaarah   bi l-baaS

c azuur   asawwi   azrag   al:ab

d daayman   kull yoom   fi s-suug   marrah fi l-usbuu:

e :ala   kam   foog   ba:d

f sawwaag at-taaksi   wasaT al-madiinah
mawgif al-baaS   markaz ash-shurTah

10 Can you complete these grammar rules correctly?

a To make the future tense, just add _____ to the present tense form of the verb.

b To say *there was* (instead of *there is*), add _____ (m) or _____ (f) in front of the word **fiih**.

c To use an imperative to a woman, add _____ to the masculine imperative.

11 Match each English statement to its correct Arabic translation.

a ista'jirna sayyáarah kabiirah	**1** He bought a new coffee pot.
b saafart ams li d-dooHah	**2** The bus went direct.
c al-baaS raja: min ad-dooHah	**3** She swam in the pool.
d sabaHat fi l-masbaH	**4** The bus returned from Doha.
e ishtara dallah jadiidah	**5** I travelled to Doha yesterday.
f raaH al-baaS mubaasharatan	**6** We hired a big car.

12 Which months are missing here?

yanaayir	_____
fibraayir	_____
_____	sabtambar
abriil	oktoobar
_____	_____
yuunyo	_____

 13 Read each sentence out loud and state whether the past (P) or future (F) tense is being used.

a saafart li-amriika yoom al-aHad.

b bitruuh al-mool yoom al-khamiis.

c bashuuf al-fiilm al-jadiid fi s-siinima.

d ishtaghal fi l-maktab aS-SubaH.

e aish biysawwi fi S-Saif?

f sharabna :aSiir fii maT:am.

 AL-KHATT AL-:ARABI *THE ARABIC SCRIPT*

Now you are more familiar with Arabic script, practise the reading skills you have developed throughout *Get Started in Arabic* by looking at these authentic Arabic signs and answering the following questions.

14 Read this travel sign and complete the sentence.

The next bus/boat/train leaves in two minutes.

15 What would you buy here?

  a medicine   **b** shoes   **c** train tickets?

16 This shop has a sale. But what's the offer?
  a 10% discount
  b three for price of two
  c buy one, get one free

17 This toy shop is having a sale. What discount is available?
  a 10–20%
  b 20–50%
  c 25–50%

18 You need to report an accident – which of these words says *Police*?

a

b

19 You and a friend are sitting in a café. Your friend does not read Arabic so it's up to you to read the menu and answer your friend's questions (prices are in UAE dirhams).
  a How much is a large iced cappuccino?
  b How much is a small iced cappuccino 'supreme'?
  c Which size smoothie costs 16 dirhams?

كبير	وسط	صغير	المشروبات الباردة
			مثلجات
١٨	١٦	١٤	كابوتشينو مثلج
٢١	١٩	١٧	كابوتشينو مثلج سوبريم
			ما فضله من النكهات
١٨	١٦	١٤	سموثي بالفواكه الطبيعية

20 Look at the opening days and times for this shopping mall, then decide whether each statement is true (T) or false (F).

a The mall opens at 9 a.m. every day.
b It closes at 10 p.m. Sunday to Wednesday.
c It closes at 11 p.m. on Saturday.

ساعات العمل:

الأحد - الأربعاء

١٠ صباحاً - ١٠ مساءً

الخميس - السبت

١٠ صباحاً - ١٢ منتصف الليل

You have now successfully completed
Get Started in Arabic.

alf mabruuk! *Congratulations!*

Answer key

PRONUNCIATION

Moon letters – a, c, d (al-kháali), f (al-áwsaT), h, j
Sun letters – b, d (ar-rúb:), e, f (ash-sharq), g, i

UNIT 1

The Arabian Gulf

(al-)lúghah

Conversation 1

1 morning
2 a no; **b** Dubai
3 a3; **b**4; **c**1; **d**5; **e**2

Language discovery

a there is no Arabic word for *is* or *are*
b ínta is the form used when speaking to a man. **ínti** is the form used when speaking to a woman
c There are three different endings: **-i, -ak, -ich** (indicates different people)

Now your turn!

ána ísm-i [your name]

Now your turn!

ána min ustráalya

Practice 1

1 a ísm-i; **b** min; **c** gáTar; **d**
2 -ich; -i; ínta; -ak; -ak; ínti
3 a ísm-i; **b** ísm-ak; **c** ána; **d** ínta; **e** Háal-ich

Listen and understand

1 a5 **b**2 **c**1 **d**6 **e**4 **f**3
2 a m; **b** f; **c** f; **d** m; **e** f; **f** m

Conversation 2

1 Mark: England; Sara: America
2 London
3 a3; b4; c5; d2; e1

Language discovery

1 **húwwa** means *he*; **híyya** means *she*
2 **háadha** means *this* when referring to a man; **háadhi** means *this* when referring to a woman

Practice 2

1 a húwwa; **b** híyya; **c** híyya; **d** húwwa
2 a háadhi fáaTimah; **b** híyya min ábu DHábi?; **c** laa, híyya min gáTar.
3 a m; **b** m; **c** m; **d** f; **e** f; **f** m
4 a háadha málik, húwwa min másqat; **b** háadha náasir, húwwa min jáddah; **c** háadhi Híbah, híyya min al-yáman; **d** háadhi maría, híyya min isbáanya

Reading Arabic

1 Read the Arabic from right to left.

4 السُّودان   3 العِرَاق   1الكُويت

1 Kuwait **2** Iraq **3** Sudan
2 1 as-sudáan; **2** :umáan; **3** al-yáman; **4** al-:iráaq; **5** al-baHráin; **6** qáTar
3 they appear at the beginning of each (reading from right to left)

Test yourself

1 a w :aláikum as-saláam; **b** masáa' an-núur; **c** ísm-i ...; **d** ána min...; **e** má:a s-saláamah
2 a :aláikum; **b** wa; **c** min; **d** ána; **e** SabáaH or masáa'; **f** kaif; **g** háadhi or ísm-i
3 a aish ísm-ich; **b** aish ísm-ak; **c** kaif Háal-ak

UNIT 2

Arabic numbers

9, 3, 1, 2

Vocabulary builder

1 a5; **b**6; **c**4; **d**2; **e**1; **f**3; **g**7
2 a Arabic; **b** English; **c** Spanish; **d** French

New expressions

Arabic, English, English, English

Conversation 1

1 Emirati

Now your turn!

c hit the brakes immediately!
2 a Do you speak English? **b** only Arabic; **c** she speaks it very well; **d** laa;
e Lauren; **f** Alex
3 a F, he speaks Arabic; **b** T; **c** F, he is Emirati

Language discovery

1 Nasser is describing himself so he uses the masculine form, -**i**. Lauren is
describing herself so she uses the feminine form, -**íyyah**.
2 a a-takállam; **b** ta-takállam; **c** ta-takallam-íin

Practice 1

1 a m; **b** f; **c** m; **d** f; **e** f; **f** m; **g** m; **h** f
2 a ingliz-íyyah; **b** ínti iTal-íyyah; **c** híyya :umaan-íyyah; **d** híyya sudaan-
íyyah; **e** ána briTaan-íyyah; **f** ínti gaTar-íyyah
3 a I am English, from London. **b** Are you Italian? **c** He is Omani. **d** He is
Sudanese. **e** I am British, from Scotland. **f** Are you Qatari?
4 a2; **b**3; **c**1
5 ínta, inglíizi, min, laa, laa, wáajid zain, shwáyya

Listen and understand

2 a 3; **b** 5; **c** 1; **d** 4; **e** 6; **f** 2
3 1 ána amríik-i; **2** ána iskutlánd-i; **3** ána inglíiz-i; **4** ána ustráal-i;
5 ána kuwait-íyyah; **6** ána farans-íyyah

Conversation 2

1 a kam rágam tilifóon-ak? **b** rágam tilifóon-i
2 a T; **b** T; **c** F-521708

Practice 2

1 e, d, b, f, c, a
2 2; 10; 3; 7; 6; 1; 5
4 a zero, seven; **b** Britain, the Emirates; **c** France, Egypt; **d** Ireland, please
5 a Bahraini (f) **b** English (f) **c** Omani (m) **d** Emirati (m) **e** Qatari (f)
f French (m)
6 a2 Fadia - Yemen; **b**4 Sausan - Saudi Arabia; **c**5 Hamdan - Iraq;
d6 Mohammed - Qatar; **e**3 Noor - Emirates; **f**1 Saif - Oman

Reading Arabic

1 a3; **b**5; **c**1; **d**2; **e**4

2 a4; **b**1; **c**5; **d**2; **e**3

Test yourself

1 a inglíiz-i; **b** farans-íyyah; **c** gátar-i; **d** kuwait-íyyah; **e** iskutláand-i;
f baHrain-íyyah

2 a sáb:ah; **b** thaláathah; **c** tís:ah; **d** wáaHid; **e** síttah; **f** ithnáin;
g khámsah; **h** :ásharah

3 a Sífir, khámsah, khámsah – ithnáin, thamáanyah, árba:ah – thaláathah,
wáaHid, thaláathah, árba:ah.

b Sífir, síttah, wáaHid, thamáanyah, thaláathah, sáb:ah, árba:ah, tís:ah,
tís:ah.

c Sífir, árba:ah, sáb:ah, khámsah, wáaHid, síttah, ithnáin, thamáanyah,
wáaHid.

UNIT 3

Getting to know Arabs

coffee, tea

Vocabulary builder

girls/daughters; sisters

New expressions

woman, woman, work

Now your turn!

a-shtághal fii mádrasah

Conversation 1

1 Sally lives in Dubai; no, she does not work

2 a nurse; **b** (big) company in Abu Dhabi; **c** bank

3 a wain ti-skun-íin al-Hiin? **b** ná-skun fii másqaT. **c** ... láakin níHna min
Suur. **d** aish ti-shtaghal-íin? **e** ána mumárriDHah. **f** ána maa a-shtághal.

Language discovery

1 níHna, íntu

Now your turn!

2 a I work; **b** you work (f); **c** he works

Now your turn!

Arabic (singular)	English	Arabic (plural)	English
(ána) a-shtághal	*I work*	(níHna) na-shtághal	*we work*
(ínta) ti-shtághal	*you(m) work*	(íntu) ti-shtaghal-úun	*you(pl) work (m/f)*
(ínti) ti-shtaghal-íin	*you(f) work*		
(húwwa) yi-shtághal	*he works*	(húmma) yi-shtaghal-úun	*they work (m/f)*
(híyya) ti-shtághal	*she works*		

Now your turn!

(húwwa) yi-shtághal fii shárikah

Practice 1

1 a húmma; **b** ínti; **c** ána; **d** íntu
2 a yi-shtághal; **b** ti-shtághal; **c** a-shtághal; **d** yi-shtaghal-úun
3 a mudárrisah; **b** Tabíib; **c** mikáaniki; **d** muhándisah
4 ána muhándis wa a-shtághal fii shárikah

Listen and understand

1 a engineer; **b** doctor; **c** student; **d** teacher; **e** mechanic;
f company director
2 a teacher; **b** bank; **c** live; **d** work; **e** work; **f** work
3 a fem; **b** masc; **c** masc; **d** fem; **e** fem; **f** masc
4 a singular; **b** plural; **c** plural; singular

Conversation 2

1 2 children; 9 and 5 years old
2 a three **b** six **c** five years old
3 a :índ-ich awláad?; **b** bass; **c** níHna :índ-na síttah

Language discovery

1 thaláath banáat
2 his and her age

Practice 2

1 a banáat; **b** ikhwáan; **c** akhawáat

2 a awláad, banáat; **b** sanawáat; **c** akhawáat

3 a -ha; **b** -uh; **c** -hum

a my daughter is seven years old; **b** my brother is six years old;
c the boys/children are three and eight years old

Reading Arabic

a5; **b**6; **c**1; **d**8; **e**7; **f**4; **g**2; **h**3

Test yourself

1 a housewife (literally master (f) of the house)

2 a Nizwa, Oman; **b** 20; **c** engineer; **d** three

3 a :úmr-i; **b** ti-shtaghal-íin; **c** :úmr-uh; **d** tí-skun; **e** yi-shtághal

REVIEW 1–3

1 c

2 a5; **b**7; **c**1; **d**3; **e**6; **f**2; **g**4

3 a ínti; **b** ínta; **c** ínta; **d** ínti

4 a3; **b**1; **c**4; **d**5; **e**2

5 a5; **b**4; **c**2; **d**1; **e**3

6 a ingliz-íyyah; **b** gaTar-íyyah; **c** Tabíib-ah; **d** mudárris-ah; **e** amriik-íyyah

7 a I am English; **b** I am Qatari; **c** I am a doctor; **d** I am a teacher;
e I am American

8 a ithnáin	2	٢
b :áshara	10	١٠
c khámsah	5	٥
d thaláathah	3	٣
e sába:ah	7	٧
f wáaHid	1	١
g thamáanyah	8	٨

9 a ána ísm-i…; **b** ána min …; **c** á-skun fii …; **d** ná:am/laa; **e** ragam
tilifóon-i …; **f** a-shtághal al-Hiin fii …; **g** ná:am :índ-i…/laa, ma :ind-i
awláad

10 a

11 a the second word; **b** al-baríid

UNIT 4

Hours of the day

2 (Monday), 4 (Wednesday), 5 (Thursday)]

Vocabulary builder

p.m. (evening)

New expressions

three; open; open; closed; ashkúr-ich

Conversation 1

1 four hours
2 7.30
3 half an hour
4 if there is one, when it closes in evening

Language discovery

1 as-sáa:ah sáb:ah
2 húwwa magfúul al-Hiin

Practice 1

1 a 4:15; b 4:40; c 8:30; d 11:05; e 2:25
2 a as-sáa:ah khámsah; b as-sáa:ah :ásharah wa nuSS; c as-sáa:ah
thaláathah ílla rúba:; d as-sáa:ah wáaHidah wa nuSS wa khams;
e as-sáa:ah sáb:ah wa thilth; f as-sáa:ah ithná:shar ílla :áshar
3 a maftúH; b maftúHah; c magfúul; d maftúH; e magfúulah

Listen and understand

1 a 8:00; b 9:30; c 4:05; d 3:45; e 7:10; f 11.55
3 as-sáa:ah ...

Conversation 2

1 post office
2 closed (all day) on Friday
3 yes
4 all day every day until midnight

Language discovery

1 magfúul yoom al-júma:ah
2 c Saturday evening
3 it closes at 12 o'clock at night

Now your turn!

a al-másbaH yí-ftaH as-sáa:ah kam yoom al-árba:ah aS-Súbah?
b al-máT:am yi-bánnid as-sáa:ah kam yoom as-sabt fi l-lail?

Practice 2

1

a al-bank yí-ftaH as-sáa:ah kam?
yí-ftaH as-sáa:ah thamáanyah aS-SúbaH.
b al-mool yí-ftaH as-sáa:ah kam?
yí-ftaH as-sáa:ah tís:ah aS-SúbaH.
c as-síinima ti-bánnid as-sáa:ah kam?
ti-bánnid as-sáa:ah iHdá:ashr wa nuSS fi l-lail.
d márkaz ash-shúrTah yí-ftaH as-sáa:ah kam?
yí-ftaH as-sáa:ah sáb:ah wa rúba: aS-SúbaH.
e ad-dukkáan yi-bánnid as-sáa:ah kam?
yi-bánnid as-sáa:ah wáaHdah wa nuSS ba:d aDH-DHuhr.
2 a 11:30; **b** 9:10; **c** 7:25; **d** 12:15; **e** 15:00; **f** 23:55
3 7 a.m. to 11 p.m.

Reading Arabic

1 a E; **b** B; **c** M, E; **d** M; **e** M; **f** B; **g** M; **h** E

Test yourself

1

a as-sáa:ah thamáanyah aS-SubaH
b as-sáa:ah thintain wa nuSS ba:d aDH-DHuhr
c as-sáa:ah síttah wa :áshar fi l-lail
d as-sáa:ah árba:ah ba:d aDH-DHuhr
e as-sáa:ah :ásharah ílla rúba: aS-SubaH
f as-sáa:ah khámsah wa rúba: fi l-lail
g as-sáa:ah sáb:ah wa nuSS aS-SubaH
h as-sáa:ah iHdá:ashar wa thilth fi l-lail

2

a yoom ath-thaláathah
b yoom as-sabt
c yoom al-khamíis
d yoom al-júma:ah
e yoom al-ithnáin
f yoom al-áHad

UNIT 5

Shopping

How much is the khanjar (dagger)?

Conversation 1

1 incense burner
2 a F; **b** T; **c** T; **d** F
3 a6; **b**4; **c**1; **d**5; **e**3; **f**2

Language discovery

a ákbar; **b** a-ríid; a-shúuf

Practice 1

1 a4; **b**2; **c**6; **d**1; **e**3; **f**5
2 new incense burner, frankincense, big shirt, old ring
3 a :índ-ak tháani áSghar?
b :índ-ak tháaniyah árkhaS?
c :índ-ak tháani áTwal?
d :índ-ak tháaniyah ágSar?
4 a postcard; **b** coffee pot; **c** beautiful bracelet;
d cheap watch; **e** bigger shirt; **f** longer necklace

Conversation 2

1 5 riyals
2 a tamáam, riyaaláin; **b** fiih :índ-ak tháani árkhaS?;
c ti-sáwwi takhfíiDH?; **d** háadha bi-thaláathah riyáal;
e kill shay gháali!; **f** shay tháani?
3 a too expensive; **b** still too expensive;
c everything is expensive; **d** two riyals

Language discovery

1 al-áHmar
2 riyaaláin

Numbers 30 to 1,000,000

(a) The Arabian Nights (lit. (a) thousand nights and (a) night]
(b) Ali Baba and the Forty Thieves

Practice 2

1 a Hámra; **b** burtugáali; **c** ákhDHar; **d** áswad; **e** zárga
2 a6; **b**1; **c**5; **d**3; **e**7; **f**2; **g**4
3 a3; **b**4; **c**5; **d**1; **e**2

Reading Arabic

1 a 5E; **b** 7M; **c** 2B; **d** 8B and M; **e** 3E; **f** 1M and M; **g** 4M; **h** 6M and M

Test yourself

as-saláamu :aláikum; a-ríid a-shtári silsílah; :índ-ak tháaniyah áTwal; shúkran. híyya jadíidah; háadhi bikám; háadhi gháaliyah; bíshtari

UNIT 6

Food and drink

a mashruubáat c sandwíicháat

Vocabulary builder

milk, sugar, juice, with, cola

Conversation 1

1 tea
2 a3; **b**4; **c**1; **d**2
3 aT; **b**F; **c**T; **d**T; **e**F

Language discovery

1 a aish :índ-kum min mashrubáat?; **b** :índ-na gáhwah
2 a ána a-Híbb :aSíir; **b** ána maa a-Híbb shaay; **c** ána a-fáDHDHal gáHwah

Practice 1

1 a6; **b**3; **c**10; **d**2; **e**1; **f**8; **g**9; **h**4; **i**7; **j**5
2 a6; **b**5; **c**2; **d**3; **e**1; **f**4
3 a2; **b**4; **c**1; **d**3

Listen and understand

1c; **2**f; **3**b; **4**a; **5**d; **6**e
2 a i; **b** ii; **c** ii; **d** ii

New expressions

falafel, houmous, cake

Now your turn!

ána jaw:áan! ána áa-khudh bárgar wa chibs, min fáDHlak.

Conversation 2

1 chicken salad with chips, cheese sandwich, burger, bread with houmus
3 a3; **b**5; **c**2; **d**1; **e**4

Language discovery

1 íntu jaw:aan-íin?
2 aish ti-riid-úun?
3 aish ti-ríid?
4 ti-riid-úun khubz?

Practice 2

1 a5; **b**3; **c**6; **d**1; **e**2; **f**4
2 a cheese sandwich; **b** burger and chips/fries; **c** falafel and hummus
3 a2; **b**3; **c**1
4 a4; **b**5; **c**2; **d**6; **e**1; **f**3
5 a íntu :aTshaan-íin? **b** aish ti-riid-úun ti-shrib-úun? **c** ti-faDHDHal-úun
gáhwah aw shaay? **d** bi-Halíib aw bi-súkkar? **e** ti-riid-úun sandwíich?
f bi-l-jíbin aw bi-d-dajáaj?

Reading Arabic

1 aM; **b**B; **c**E; **d**M; **e**B; **f**M; **g**M; **h**E
a6 qáTar (Qatar)
a7 Táyyib (fine)
c4 qamíiS (shirt)
d6 aDH-DHahráan (Dhahran, a city in Saudi Arabia)]
e1 ábu DHábi (Abu Dhabi)
f3 báiDHah (egg)
g2 áSfar (yellow)
h5 HooD (tank)
3 a3 restaurant; **b**1 exit only; **c** 2 no photography

Test yourself

a masáa' an-nuur. aish :índ-kum min mashruubáat? **b** aish :índ-kum min
:aSíir? **c** ána báa-khudh :aSíir Tuffáh. aish :índ-kum min sandwiicháat?
d a:Tíini bárgar wa baTáaTa. **e** laa, bidúun SálaTah. **f** shúkran

1 a thaláathah; **b** wa; **c** sáb:ah, nuSS; **d** ílla

2 a a.m. **b** p.m. **c** p.m. **d** a.m.

3 fiih másbaH (hína) fi l-fúndug?

4 a6; **b**3; **c**4; **d**7; **e**1; **f**5; **g**2

5 a as-síinima tíftaH as-sáa:ah kam?

b al-máT:am yibánnid as-sáa:ah kam?

c al-mool yíftaH as-sáa:ah tís:ah wa nuss.

d al-másbaH yibánnid as-sáa:ah sáb:ah fi l-lail.

6 a ٥٣ (53); **b** ٤٥ (45); **c** ٢٣٠ (230); **d** ٢٩ (29); **e** ٨٧ (87); **f** ٢٠٠٠ (2000)

7 a masculine - húwwa, háadha

b feminine - híyya, háadhi

8 a M – ring; **b** F – necklace, chain; **c** M – incense burner; **d** F – card;

e M – dress; **f** M – shirt

9 a wrong – háadhi zoolíyyah jamíilah.

b correct

c wrong – háadha finjáan rakhíiS.

d wrong – háadhi silsílah Tawíilah.

a This is a beautiful carpet.

b This is a big incense burner.

c This is a cheap coffee cup.

d This is a long necklace.

10 a4 big; **b**3 small; **c**5 cheap; **d**6 expensive; **e**1 short; **f**2 tall; **g**7 beautiful

11

:índ-ak tháani ákbar

:índ-ak tháani áSghar

:índ-ak tháani árkhaS

:índ-ak tháani ághla

:índ-ak tháani ágSar

:índ-ak tháani áTwal

:índ-ak tháani ájmal

12

a :índ[-i]	*I have*	
b :índ[-uh]	*he has*	
c :índ[-na]	*we have*	
d :índ[-hum]	*they have*	
e :índ[-ich]	*you (f) have*	

13 a4; **b**1; **c**2; **d**3

14 a-ríid/áa-khudh/a:Tíini:

a :aSíir laimóon bi súkkar

b sandwíich wa kóola

c gáhwah wa kaik

a-Híbb (I like), maa a-Híbb (I don't like)

15

a al-fúndug- others are days

b thaláathah - others are multiples of ten

c zoolíyyah - others are colours

d :aSíir laimóon - others are foods

16 c (speed limit is 50)

17 a D3; **b** G4; **c** H7; **d** A8; **e** F2; **f** E1; **g** B6; **h** C5

UNIT 7

Getting around the city

fish market

Vocabulary builder

mosque, supermarket, fish market

left, right

Conversation 1

1 go straight on

2 a4; **b**3; **c**1; **d**2

3 a laa, maa á:raf; **b** ruuH síidah; **c** ba:dáin liff yamíin;

d al-bank ba:íid :an hína

4 a F; **b** T; **c** T; **d** F – five minutes away

Language discovery

1 fiih baríid garíib min hína?laa, maa fiih.

2 ruuH síidah

Practice 1

1 fúndug, márkaz ash-shúrTah, máT:am, Saydalíyyah, mustáshfa

2 a3; **b**1; **c**2

3 a4; **b**1; **c**2; **d**3

4 a liff; **b** ruuH; **c** liff

5 a fiih baríid garíib min hína?

b fiih mustáshfa garíibah min hína?

c fiih márkaz ash-shúrTah garíib min hína?

d fiih mátHaf garíib min hína?

e fiih fúndug garíib min hína?

f fiih Saydalíiyyah garíibah min hína?

g fiih mádrasah garíibah min hína?

h fiih suug as-sámak garíib min hína?

6 a al-baríid ba:íid :an hína?

b al-mustáshfa ba:íidah :an hína?

c al-márkaz ash-shúrTah ba:íid :an hína?

d al-mátHaf ba:íid :an hína?

e al-fúndug ba:íid :an hína?

f aS-Saydalíiyyah ba:íidah :an hína?

g al-mádrasah ba:íidah :an hína?

Listen and understand

1 a hospital ✓; **b** hotel ✗; **c** market ✗; **d** shop ✓; **e** museum ✗; **f** cinema ✓; **g** pharmacy ✓

2 a C2; **b** D4; **c** A3; **d** B1

New expressions

hotel, hotel, right, left

Conversation 2

1 fúndug ash-shams (lit. Sun Hotel)

2 Don't speed up!

3 straight, roundabout, right, second, right, 50, restaurant

Language discovery

a khudh tháani sháari: :ála l-yamíin; **b** jamb máT:am al-khalíij

Practice 2

1 a 3; **b** 7; **c** 1; **d** 5; **e** 8; **f** 4; **g** 2; **h** 6

2 a khudh áwwal sháari: :ála l-yamíin; **b** khudh tháalith sháari: :ála l-yisáar; **c** khudh ráabi: sháari: :ála l-yamíin wa ba:dáin liff yisáar; **d** khudh tháani sháari: :ála l-yamíin wa ba:dáin ruuH síidah; **e** :ind ad-duwwáar liff yisáar

3 a khúdhi áwwal sháari: :ála l-yamíin; **b** khúdhi tháalith sháari: :ála l-yisáar; **c** khúdhi ráabi: sháari: :ála l-yamíin wa ba:dáin líffi yisáar; **d** khúdhi tháani sháari: :ála l-yamíin wa ba:dáin rúuHi síidah; **e** :ind ad-duwwáar líffi yisáar

4 a pharmacy; **b** go straight, at the roundabout turn right; **c** on the left; **d** next to the restaurant

5 a al-wálad fi l-máT:am, b as-síinima ba:d márkaz ash-shúrTah, c al-baríid gábil as-subermáarkit, d aS-Saydalíyyah jamb al-mátHaf, e as-sayyáarah taHt al-jisr, f al-fúndug ba:d al-másjid

Reading Arabic

1 a street; **b** lúghah; **c** on; **d** after; **e** :aSíir; **f** expensive; **g** :umáan; **h** Baghdad

2 :árabi (Arabic)

4 a 2 **b** 1

Test yourself

1 samáHt, wain, rúuH, yamíin, tháani, :ála, ba:d, as-suug, fiih, maa

2 a fiih máT:am garíib min hína **b** al-báHar min wain **c** kaif arúuH as-síinima min hína

3 a ruuH síidah; **b** líffi yisáar wa ba:dáin rúuHi síidah; **c** ruuH síidah wa ba:dáin khudh tháani sháari: :ála l-yamíin; **d** laa, maa fiih bank garíib min hína; **e** suug as-sámak jamb al-míina

UNIT 8

Getting out and about

a mitru; **b** mawgif al-baaS

Vocabulary builder

taxi, metro

New expressions

bus, two, plane

Conversation 1

1 return

2 a false – 125 riyals; **b** false – 8 a.m.; true

3 a fiih baaS yiruuH mubaasharatan; **b** at-tadhkarah bi-kam? **c** al-baaS yiTla: as-saa:ah kam?; **d** mata yoosal ad-dooHah?; **e** a:Tiini tadhkarat dhihaab w iyaab Hagg baakir.

Language discovery

1 a:Tiini tadhkarat dhihaab w iyaab
2 fiih baaS yiruuH ad-dooHah min faDHlak?

Practice 1

1 a3; b5; c4; d1; e2
2 a yiruuH; b mubaasharatan; c bi-kam; d iyaab; e yiTla::; f mata;
g as-saa:ah; h Hagg
3 a True; b False (arrives in Sohar at 1005); c False (not direct);
d True
4 a 4; b 5; c2; d3; e1

Listen and understand

1 a return; b one-way; c return; d one-way
2 a fiih baaS yiruuH abu DHabi; b fiih baaS yiruuH masqat; c fiih baaS
yiruuH ar-riyaaDH; d fiih baaS yiruuH Salalah.
3 SabaaH al-khair.
fiih giTaar yiruuH ar-riyaaDH baakir ba:d aDH-DHuhr?
yiTla: as-saa:ah kam?
yooSal as-saa:ah kam fi r-riyaaDH?
tádhkarat thiháab w iyáab bikam?

New expressions

four-wheel drive/4x4; day; days

Conversation 2

1 4W drive
2 a new, very nice/beautiful; b does it have A/C; c two days; d 300 Dh;
e yes; f Saturday 4 p.m.
3 a hiyya sayyaarah waajid jamiilah; b dagiigah min faDHlak; c yoom
as-sabt, nafs al-wagt; d as-saa:ah kam laazim arajji:ha

Language discovery

a :ishriin laitir mumtaaz; b mumkin tichayyik al-aayil?

Practice 2

a4; b3; c2; d5; e1

Reading Arabic

a4; b3; c2; d1

Test yourself

a fiih baaS yiruuH abu DHabi?
b mata yooSal?
c tadhkarat dhihaab (bass) bi-kam?
d :Tiini tadhkarat dhihaab w iyaab
e ariid asta'jir sayyaarah min faDHlak.
f kam al-iijaar li-usbuu: waaHid?
g mumkin adfa: bi l-kart?

UNIT 9

Leisure

Do you like football?

Vocabulary builder

music, squash, cinema, television, football

Conversation 1

1 football
2 a2; b3; c1
3 a4; b5; c1; d2; e3
4 **a** False – he plays with friends; **b** False – he doesn't like football; **c** True;
d False – Thursday

Language discovery

a marrtain fi l-usbuu:; **b** aHyaanan; **c** aruuH al:ab; **d** nijlis fi l-bait; **e** bashuufak

Now your turn!

a aHyaanan; **b** kull or kill; **c** marrah; **d** daayman; **e** ba:d

Practice 1

1 a5; b6; c9; d2; e3; f7; g8; h1; i4
2 a3; b5; c1; d2; e6; f4
3 a3; b4; c5; d2; e1
4 **a**4 bitruuH; **b**3 biyruuH; **c**2 bashuuf; **d**1 binsawwi

Listen and understand

1
a tennis – every day after work
b cinema – twice a month
c beach (with friends) – sometimes
d mall – always on Thursdays
e market – never

2 sometimes (aHyaanan), with friends (Sadiigaat), shopping (aruuH as-suug) cinema (as-siinima), sport (ar-riyaaDHah), swimming (as-sibaaHah), I don't like (maa aHibb), in shaa 'Al-laah

3 a5; **b**4; **c**1; **d**2; **e**3

New expressions

do you think, tomorrow

Conversation 2

1 to visit Salma and Shamsa

2 a go to the mall; **b** going day after tomorrow (with sister); **c** visit Salma and Shamsah; **d** 10 o'clock

Language discovery

a wain tiriidiin tiruuHiin; b tiriidiin tiruuHiin al-mool?; c mumkin nruuH nzuur salma wa shamsa

Practice 2

1

a aruuH ashuuf fiilm fi s-siinima.

b aruuH amshi :ala l-baHar.

c aruuH azuur ahl-ii fii sidaab

d aruuH al:ab goolf ma: Sadiig-i.

e aruuH agra' fi l-Hadiiqah

f aruuH at:allam al-lughah al-yabaaniyyah.

2 There are various possibilities – Q1 supplies suggested answers.

Now your turn!

as-saa:ah khamsah munaasib l-ak?

Reading Arabic

1 a laam and waaw; **b** miim; **c** miim, waaw, laam; **d** miim (appears twice); **e** laam; **f** waaw, laam, meem, haa'

2 a as-suuq; **b** maktab; **c** dubay mool; **d** mumtaaz; **e** Haliib; **f** doorat al-miyah

Test yourself

1 a Hibb/maa aHibb a al-ghooS; **b** ar-riyaaDah; **c** as-sibaaHah; **d** at-takhayyam

2 a ana bal:ab kurah; **b** niHna binal:ab skwaash; **c** inta bitshuuf at-tilifizyoon; **d** huwwa biyruuH al-mool

3 The answers for this depend on your own preferences.

4 laa, ana faaDHi.
mumkin nal:ab kurah :ala l-baHar.
as-saa:ah khamsah
ashuuf-ak baakir in shaa' Al-laah
ma:a as-salaamah

UNIT 10

Holiday time

a min máayo li sabtámbar; **b** ijáazat aS-Saif

Vocabulary builder

April, August, December

New expressions

year, first, we, I, plane, car, I, we

Conversation 1

1 The Emirates and Oman
2 a5; **b**1; **c**4; **d**2; **e**3
3 a T; **b** F; **c** F – visited museums in Sharjah; **d** T
4 a iii; **b** i; **c** iv

Language discovery

a ruHt; **b** shufna; **c** sawwaina; **d** zurt

Now your turn!

a la:bt, sáafart, rája:t, takállamt, ishtághalt, sábaHt, shárabt
b la:bna, sáafarna, rája:na, takállamna, ishtághalna, sábaHna, shárabna

Practice 1

1 a2; **b**3; **c**1
2 a3; **b**4; **c**5; **d**1; **e**6; **f**2
3 ams … **a** ana ruHt as-siinima; **b** huwwa sharab gahwah; **c** niHna zurna al-matHaf; **d** inti ruHti al-mool; **e** huwwa ishtaghal fi l-maktab; **f** humma raaHu suug adh-dhahab.
4 Yesterday … **a** I went to the cinema; **b** he drank coffee; **c** we visited the museum; **d** you (f) went to the shopping mall; **e** he worked in the office; **f** they went to the gold market.
5 a F; **b** F; **c** T; **d** NT; **e** F; **f** T; **g** F
6 a with her sister **b** her sister bought new clothes; **e** her brother visited the Sheikh Zayed Grand Mosque; **g** her friend Charlotte visited the water park

8

	morning	afternoon
a	went to shopping mall	visited parents
b	watched TV in the house	worked in the office
c	visited sister Fatima	went to cinema with husband
d	played football with friends	went on trip to beach

Conversation 2

1 a2; **b**5; **c**4; **d**1; **e**3

2 a

3 c

4 b

5 a kaan al-jaww Haarr; **b** kaan fiih bard w maTar; **c** kunt fii brizban yoomain bass

Now your turn!

1 a kunt fi d- dooHah al-usbuu: al-maaDHi; **b** kaan al maT:am magfuul yoom al-juma:ah; **c** kaan al-fiilm waajid zain; **d** kaan :induh bait kabiir fii landan; **e** kaan fiih waajid naas fi s-suug ams

Practice 2

1 a3; **b**6; **c**5; **d**1; **e**2; **f**4

2 a kaan al-jaww baarid; **b** kaan fiih maTar; **c** kaan fiih Harr; **d** kaan al-jaww muu zain; **e** kaan fiih thalj; **f** kaan al-jaww baarid

3 a3; **b**4; **c**1; **d**5; **e**6; **f**2

Reading Arabic

1

a Something to eat - as-samak (fish) السمك

b Something to drink - al-qahwah (coffee) القهوة

c A way to travel - bi s-sayyaraah (by car) بالسيارة

d A day of the week - sabt (Saturday) سبت

2 a fish; **b** coffee; **c** car; **d** Saturday

3 a ana uHibbu s-samak

b ashrabu l-qahwah kull yoom

c saafartu ila dubay bi s-sayyaarah

d al-maT:am maftuuH kull yoom sabt

4 a I like fish; **b** I drink coffee every day; **c** I travelled to Dubai by car; **d** The restaurant is open every Saturday

Test yourself

1 a shuft at-tilifizyoon; **b** sharabt (finjaan) gahwah; **c** la:bt tanis; **d** ruHt as-siinima

REVIEW UNITS 7–10

1 a6; b5; c2; d1; e4; f3

2 a cinema

b football

c swimming and diving

d squash

e meeting up or going to the market with friends

f music, staying at home, watching TV

3 a law samaHt, al-baHar min wain?

b law samaHti, as-suug min wain?

c law samaHti, aS-Saydaliiyah min wain?

d law samaHt, al-maTaar min wain?

e law samaHt, al-bank min wain?

f law samaHti, as- as-súubermarkit min wain?

4 fiih; maa fiih

5 a4; b1; c6; d5; e3; f2

6 i, d, a, g, e, h, c, f, b

7 a kurah; **b** jalsah; **c** sibaaHah; **d** musiiga; **e** siinima; **f** aruuH al-mool

8 a al-jaww zain al-yoom

b kaif al-jaww fi l-baHrain?

c kaan al-jaww baarid

d kaan fiih maTar aS-SubaH

e darajat il-Haraarah sittah wa thalaathiin

9 a falaafil (the others are weather)

b bi-sukkar (the others are transport)

c azrag (the others are verbs in the I–form)

d fi s-suug (the others are time adverbs/phrases)

e kam (the others are prepositions)

f sawwaag at-taaksi (the others are places in town)

10 a b-(or bi-); **b** kaan (m), kaanat (f); **c** -i

11 a 6; **b** 5; **c** 4; **d** 3; **e** 1; **f** 2

12 mars, maayo, yuulyo, aghusTos, nufambar, disambar

13 a P; **b** F; **c** F; **d** P; **e** f; **f** P

14 train

15 a medicine (Saydaliyyah is *a pharmacy*)
16 b
17 c 25 to 50 per cent
18 a shurTah
19 a 18 dirhams; **b** 17 dirhams; **c** medium
20 a F - opens at 10 a.m.; **b** T; **c** F - closes at midnight on Saturday

Core vocabulary

:áa'ilah (pl. -áat)	family
:áadi	regular (petrol), normal
:ála	on
:ámal	work (noun)
:arábi/-íyyah	Arab/Arabic (m/f)
:aSíir	juice
:aTsháan	thirsty
:ind	at, by, with (used for to have)
:umáan	Oman
:úmr	life, age
ab (also wáalid)	father
ábadan	never
ábyaDH (f. báiDHa)	white
áHmar (f. Hámra)	red
áHsan	better
aHyáanan	sometimes
áiDHan (also ba:d)	also
aish?	what?
ákbar	bigger
akh (pl. ikhwáan)	brother
akhbáar	news
ákhDHar (f. kháDHra)	green
ákil	food
ákthar	more
al-Hiin	now
al-khalíij (al-arábi)	Gulf, the (Arabian)
al-yoom	today
almáaniya	Germany
amáam	in front of
amríika	America
ams	yesterday
ána	I
áSfar (f. Sáfra)	yellow
ash-sharq/ash-sharg al-áwsaT	Middle East, the
ásra:	faster, fastest
áswad (f. sóoda)	black
aw	or
áwwal	first
áwwalan	firstly, first of all
ayy	any, which?
ázraq/ázrag (f. zárqa/zárga)	blue

ba:d	*after, also, still*
ba:d aDH-Dhuhr	*afternoon (lit. after the noon)*
ba:dáin	*then, afterwards, later*
báachir/báakir/búkrah	*tomorrow*
báarid	*cold (adj)*
baaS (pl. -áat)	*bus*
báHar	*sea/beach*
baHráin (al-)	*Bahrain*
báiDHah (pl. baiDH)	*egg*
bait (pl. buyúut)	*house/home*
bank (pl. bunúuk)	*bank*
bantalóon	*trousers*
bard	*cold (noun)*
bárgar, bárghar	*burger*
baríid	*post office*
bass	*only, enough*
baTáaTa	*chips/fries*
bi DH-DHábt	*exactly*
bi-	*with, by, in*
bi-dúun	*without*
bi-kháir	*well*
biláad (f) (pl. buldáan)	*country*
bint (pl. banáat)	*girl, daughter*
bi-l-Halíib (also bi-Halíib)	*with milk*
briTáaniya	*Britain*
burj (pl. abráaj)	*tower*
burtuqáali/burtuqáali/-yah	*orange (colour) (m/f)*
burtuqáal/burtugáal	*orange (fruit)*
dáayman	*always*
dagíigah (pl. dagáayig)	*minute*
dajáaj	*chicken (collective noun)*
dárajah (pl. -áat)	*degree*
dawwáar	*roundabout*
dháhab	*gold*
diháab	*single/one-way (ticket)*
DHúh(u)r	*noon*
dóorat al-miyáah	*bathrooms, restrooms*
dukkáan	*shop (small)*
fáaDHi/-yah (m/f)	*free, also empty*
faránsa	*France*
fii	*in*
fiih	*there is, there are*
fiilm (pl. afláam)	*film*
fíkrah	*idea*
finjáan (pl. fanajíin)	*coffee cup*
fooq/foog	*up, above*
fúndug/fúnduq (pl. fanáadig)	*hotel*

gháali/-yah	expensive (m/f)
ghaim	clouds
gharb	west
ghooS	diving
háadha/f. háadhi/pl. haadhóol	this, these
Haal	condition
Haarr	hot
Hagg	for
Hálaq/Hálag	earrings
Halíib	milk
Hálu/Hálwah	sweet, also great, cool (m/f)
Haráarah	heat
Harr	heat
háwa	wind
hína/híni	here
híyya	she
húmma	they
húwwa	he
illa	except
imaaráat	Emirates
imaaráat (al-)	(the) Emirates
ingiltárra	England
ingliizi/-íiyyah	English (m/f)
ínta	you (m. sing)
ínti	you (f. sing)
íntu	you (pl.)
isbáanya	Spain
iskutlánda	Scotland
iTáaliya	Italy
jábal (pl. jibáal)	mountain
jadíid/-ah	new (m/f)
jálsah	hanging out, picnic, barbecue
jamb	next to
jamíil/-ah	beautiful (m/f)
jaw:áan/-ah	hungry (m/f)
jazíilan	very much (after shukran thanks)
jib(i)n	cheese
jíddan (also wáajid)	very
jinsíiyyah (pl. -áat)	nationality
kabíir/-ah	big (m/f)
kaif?	how?
kaik	cake
kam?	how much, many?
kathíir/-ah	a lot, many/much (m/f)
khoor	creek
kídha	that sort of thing, like this/that

kill shay, also kull shay	*everything*
kill, kull	*every*
kitáab (pl. kútub)	*book*
kúrah	*football*
kuwáit (al-)	*Kuwait*
láakin	*but*
láazim	*necessary, must*
lail (general); lailah (single night)	*night*
laimóon	*lemon*
laish?	*why?*
li-	*to*
lúghah (pl. -áat)	*language*
má:a	*with, together with*
maa	*not (before verbs)*
máaDHi (-iyah)	*last (e.g. week, year) (m/f)*
maay	*water*
madíinah (pl. múdun)	*city*
madrásah (pl. madáaris)	*school*
maftúuH/-ah	*open (m/f)*
maqfúul/magfúul/-ah	*closed (m/f)*
makáan (pl. -áat)	*place*
máktab (pl. makáatib)	*office*
márkaz ash-shúrTah	*police station*
márkaz tijáari	*shopping centre*
márkib (pl. maráakib)	*boat*
márrah (pl. marráat)	*time, occasion (pl. sometimes)*
márrah tháaniyaah	*again (lit. a second time)*
márrah/marr(a)táin	*once/twice*
mása	*evening*
másbaH	*swimming pool*
mashghúul/-ah	*busy (m/f)*
mashrúub (pl. mashruubáat)	*drink*
másjid	*mosque*
máT:am (pl. maTáa:im)	*restaurant*
máta?	*when?*
maTáar	*airport*
máTar	*rain*
máthaf (pl. matáaHif)	*museum*
mawjúud/-ah	*present, here (m/f)*
máwqif/máwgif (pl. mawáaqif)	*parking*
min	*from*
mool	*shopping mall*
mubáasharatan	*directly*
mudárris/-ah)	*teacher (m/f)*
múmkin	*possible*
mumtáaz	*excellent, super, premium (petrol)*

mushkílah (pl. masháakil)	problem
musíiqa/musíiga	music
mustáshfa (f)	hospital
muu	not (before nouns and adjectives)
na:náa:	mint
níHna	we
nuSS	half
qábil/gábil	before
qadíim/gadíim/-ah	old (m/f)
qáHwah/gáhwah	coffee
qaríib/garíib/-ah	near (m/f)
qaSíir/gaSíir/-ah	short (m/f)
qáTar/gáTar	Qatar
qiTáar/giTáar (pl. -áat)	train
ra'y	opinion
rajjáal (pl. rajajíil)	man
rakhíiS/-ah	cheap (m/f)
ráqam/rágam	number
ráqam/rágam tilifóon	phone number
ríHlah (pl. -áat)	journey, trip
riyáaDHah	sport
rúba:	quarter
sáa:ah (pl. -áat)	hour, clock, watch
Sadíiq/Sadíig (pl. aSdiqáa')	friend (m)
Sadíiqah/Sadíigah (pl. -áat)	friend (f)
Saghíir/-ah	small (m/f)
Saif	summer
SálaTah	salad
sámak	fish (collective noun)
sánah (pl. sanawáat)	year
saríi:/-ah	fast (m/f)
Sayd as-sámak	fishing
Saydalíiyyah	pharmacy
sayyáarah (pl. -áat)	car
sháari:	street
shaay	tea
sháhar (pl. shuhúur)	month
shamáal	north
shams	sun
shárikah (pl. -áat)	company
sharq/sharg	east
shay (pl. ashyáa)	thing
shibs	potato crisps
shíishah/maHáTTat banzíin	petrol station
shíta	winter
shúghal	work

shwáyya	little (amount)
sí:ir	price
síidah	straight on
síinima (f)	cinema
Súb(a)H	morning
súkkar	sugar
súubermarkit	supermarket
suuq/suug (pl. aswáag)	market, souk
Táalib/-ah	student (m/f)
Tabíib/-ah	doctor (m/f)
tádhkarah (pl. tadháakir)	ticket
taH(i)t	down, under
taqríiban/tagríiban	approximately
tasáwwaq	shopping
Tawiil/-ah	long (m/f)
Tayyáarah (pl. -áat)	plane
tháani/-yah	another, second (one) (m/f)
thalj	snow, ice
tilifizyóon	television
tilifóon	mobile/telephone
ukht (pl. akhawáat)	sister
umm (also wáalidah)	mother
usbúu:	week
ustráaliya	Australia
wa	and
wáajid (also jíddan)	very, much, many
wáalid (also ab)	father
wáalidah (also umm)	mother
waalidáin	parents
wain?	where?
wálad (awláad)	boy/son (pl. also means children)
waqt/wagt al-faráagh	time/free time
wára	behind
wásaT	centre, medium, middle
yamíin	right
yiSáar (also shimáal)	left
yoom	day
zooj	husband
zóojah	wife

Useful phrases

:áfwan	you're welcome, excuse me
:an ídhnik	excuse me
áasif, áasifah	sorry
áhlan wa sáhlan	hello, welcome
as-saláamu :alaikum	hello
ashkúr-ak/-ich	thank you (formal)
áywa, also ná:am	yes
bikám?	how much? (price)
fii amáan Al-láah	goodbye (lit. May God keep you safe)
Hayyáa-k Al-láah	thank you, goodbye (lit. God give you life)
in shaa' Al-láah	God willing
khalíini afákkir	let me think
laa	no
law samáHt/-i	please, excuse me (m/f)
ma:a s-saláamah	goodbye
maa fiih	there isn't/aren't
maa sháa' Al-láah	my goodness! Wow!
min fáDHlak/-ich	please (m/f)
muu mushkílah!	no problem!
ná:am, (also áywa)	yes
nzain (also zain)	good, fine
shúkran	thank you
shwáyya	a little
shwáyya shwáyya	slowly
Tab:an	of course
tamáam	good, fine
Táyyib	OK, good, fine
tfáDHDHal/-i	here you are (m/f) (when giving something to someone)
wa :aláikum as-saláam	hello (in reply to as-saláamu :alaikum)
ya jamáa:ah	hey, everyone!
yá:ani	well, ... um, kind of
zain (also nzain)	good, well, fine

List of verbs

Here is a list of verbs which appear in *Get Started in Arabic*. In each case, the *he* form of the past tense is given first, followed by the *he* form of the present tense. Remember to note where the stress lies.

:áraf/yí:raf	to know
á:Ta/yá:Ti	to give
ákhadh/yáakhúdh	to take
aráad/yaríid	to want, wish
ashtára/yishtári	to buy
bánnad/yibánnid	it closes (m/f)
cháyyik, yicháyyik	to check
dáfa:/yídfa:	to pay
fátaH/yíftaH	it opens (m/f)
ishtághal/yishtághal	to work
ishtára/yishtári	to buy
istá'jar/yistá'jir	to rent, hire
jálas/yíjlis	to stay, sit, remain
kaan/káanat	was (m/f)
lá:ab/yíl:ab	to play
laff, yilíff	to turn (direction)
laff/yilíff	to turn to (direction)
naam/yináam	to sleep
qára/yíqra gára/yígra	to read
raaH/yirúH	to go
rajja:/yirájji:	to return something
sáafar/yisáafir	to travel
sákan/yískun	to live
sáwwa/yisáwwi	to do, make
shaaf/yishúuf	to see, look at
ta:állam/yit:állam	to learn
Tála:/yíTla:	to leave, go out
wáSal/yóoSal	to arrive
zaar/yizúur	to visit

Acknowledgements

We would like to thank the following people for their kindness to us during the writing of this book: the Battashi family, in particular Saif and Fatimah al-Battashi; Kirsty Christer, Azza al-Harthi, Larry Brown and the staff at the Center for International Learning in Muscat, for their generous assistance; Joanna Groves, Dawn and Simon Thompson, Malinka van der Gaauw, Andy Figgins, Sawad Hussain, Fionnuala Quirke, Deborah Hennigan and all friends and family for their practical and moral support. Special thanks are due to Eid Yusef and Ahmed Chbib for their invaluable contributions, support, and for always being on hand.

Many thanks, also, to all our editors at Hodder. We are grateful for all their help, patience and encouragement.

Last but by no means least, we dedicate this book to the memory of Jack Smart. It is because of his life-long commitment to the Arabic language, which has inspired so many, and his passion and enthusiasm for the countries and the people of the Arab world, that we have been able to write this book.

Frances Altorfer

Mairi Smart

Photo credits

The authors and publisher would like to thank the following people for permission to reproduce the following images:

Dawn and Simon Thompson: four-wheel vehicle on sand-dune in Unit 9.

Tamsin Hosking: Arabic coffee pot, in Unit 3

All other photographs were supplied by the authors and are the copyright of Frances Altorfer and Mairi Smart unless specified otherwise.